Consecrated for Worship

A Directory on Church Building

Consecrated for Worship

A Directory on Church Building

SEPTEMBER 2006

Catholic Bishops' Conference of England & Wales

CATHOLIC TRUTH SOCIETY
PUBLISHERS TO THE HOLY SEE

Published 2006, by the Catholic Truth Society and Colloquium (CaTEW) Ltd.
The Catholic Truth Society, 40-46 Harleyford Road, Vauxhall, London SE11 5AY;
www.cts-online.org.uk
Colloquium (CaTEW) Ltd, 39 Eccleston Square, London SW1V 1BX.
www.catholicchurch.org.uk

ISBN 1 86082 384 X

The Liturgy Office of the Bishops' Conference

The Liturgy Office works with the Bishops' Conference Department of Christian Life and Worship to provide resources to support worthy celebration of the Liturgy. It seeks to promote the full, conscious and active participation of all the baptised in the Liturgy so that they might find there the nourishment and inspiration necessary to sustain them in their Christian lives and witness.

Website: www.liturgyoffice.org.uk

Contents

Foreword

Pope Benedict XVI recently observed that:

'At the very centre of social life there must be a presence that evokes the mystery of the transcendent God. God and man walk together in history, and the role of the Temple is to provide a visible sign of this communion.'

Catechesis, 14th September, 2005

Here, the Holy Father is speaking of the Temple in Jerusalem, and the role it played in the life of Jewish society two thousand years ago. He might equally have been speaking of the role played today by the churches which are found in our own cities, towns and villages.

The beauty of their design, indeed their very existence, serve as eloquent witnesses to the whole of our society of the Gospel; of our belief in the mystery of God's saving grace and of our desire to respond to such love through lives of faithful discipleship.

Yet it is clearly important also that our churches are suited for the celebration of the sacred mysteries of the liturgy. The renewal of the liturgy called for by the Second Vatican Council has made new demands on our churches. These are still not always as well understood as they should be.

Consecrated for Worship will prove of great assistance to those charged with responsibility for implementing the work of liturgical renewal, and with the care for the Church's rich architectural patrimony.

✠ Arthur Roche
Bishop of Leeds
Chairman of the Department for Christian Life and Worship
Bishops' Conference of England and Wales

The Lord is the living stone, rejected by men but chosen by God and precious to him; set yourselves close to him so that you too, the holy priesthood that offers the spiritual sacrifices which Jesus Christ has made acceptable to God, may be living stones making a spiritual house. As scripture says: See how I lay in Zion a precious cornerstone that I have chosen and the man who rests his trust on it will not be disappointed. That means that for you who are believers, it is precious; but for unbelievers, the stone rejected by the builders has proved to be the keystone, a stone to stumble over, a rock to bring men down. They stumble over it because they do not believe in the word; it was the fate in store for them.

But you are a chosen race, a royal priesthood, a consecrated nation, a people set apart to sing the praises of God who called you out of the darkness into his wonderful light.

1 Peter 2:4-10

OVERVIEW

What is this book?

Consecrated for Worship is a teaching and policy document for the Catholic Church in England and Wales. It concerns the building, alteration, conservation and maintenance of the Church's places of worship. It assembles together material from the liturgical books of the Roman Rite and the teaching documents and guidelines of the Holy See. In addition it develops that teaching as it applies to the particular circumstances of the Church in England and Wales.

Who is this book for?

This book has been prepared to assist those involved in:

- building a new church;
- reordering an existing church;
- making alterations within a church, whether temporary or permanent;
- engaging with those bodies with statutory responsibility for listed buildings.

It will also be helpful for those responsible for preparing for the celebration of the liturgy in less permanent worship spaces that sometimes have to be provided, for example in schools.
It is a necessary resource for:

- clergy and the lay faithful;
- parishes and religious communities;
- Diocesan Liturgy Commissions and other committees charged with special responsibility for art and architecture in all diocesan churches;
- Historic Churches Committees, charged with particular responsibility for listed churches;
- architects and other professionals involved in a building or reordering project.

It addresses the different stages of such projects: the catechesis of parish decision-makers, briefing of architects, approval of plans, designs and materials, consultation with diocesan and civil authorities and the obtaining of the necessary faculty for work on listed buildings. Finally, it addresses the dedication of a new church or altar.

How is this book organised?

After the Introduction the book is divided into four principal parts:

Part One outlines the relationship between the Church which worships and the churches built to house the worship of the Church.

Part Two explains the process to be considered when building a new church or when making changes to, or reordering, an existing one.

Part Three deals with practical theology and its application. It takes areas and elements within the church in turn and gathers together the requirements and references in the various rites and documents of the Church. It sets out liturgical law and gives guidelines. This is the most practical section in the book.

In **Part Three** the various elements of a church are dealt with in separate sections. However, those concerned with the provision and ordering of sacred spaces need to think of each element in the light of the others, as all are related and form part of one single setting for the Sacred Liturgy.

Part Four outlines the need for the continuing care of our church buildings in the light of their significance both as places of Catholic worship and as forming part of the patrimony of the wider community, both local and national.

The principles set out here do not provide a blueprint for every church but offer parameters within which those responsible for each church may safely work as they seek to enable their church to best serve the worship of the Church.

Introduction

1. *Father of holiness and power,*
we give you thanks and praise
through Jesus Christ your Son.
For you have blessed this work of our hands
and your presence makes it a house of prayer;
nor do you ever refuse us welcome
when we come in before you as your pilgrim people.

In this house you realise the mystery of your dwelling among us
for in shaping us as your holy temple
you enrich your whole Church,
which is the very body of Christ,
and thus bring closer to fulfilment
the vision of your peace,
the heavenly city of Jerusalem...

Preface of the Dedication of a Church in use,
Rite of Dedication of a Church and an Altar (RDC)

2. *From age to age you gather a people to yourself...*

Eucharistic Prayer III, *Roman Missal* (RM)

This work of our hands

3. The Church is called to be the Mystical Body of Christ on earth, a pilgrim people with no abiding city. (cf. *Sacrosanctum Concilium* (SC) 2, 7) Yet church buildings are part of everyone's life, whether believer or not. In every community, the churches are as varied in character as the congregations that use them. Catholic churches witness to the faith of past generations even as they serve the faith of contemporary congregations. They are places where personal, family and community memories mingle. They should also speak powerfully of the ongoing life and vitality of the Church, and support the Church's present need to evangelise in contemporary society.

The Bishops recognise the need for good stewardship of this rich patrimony. They exercise this responsibility through their Diocesan Liturgy Commissions and Art and Architecture Committees, and in the case of listed churches through diocesan and interdiocesan Historic Churches Committees.

4. The relationship between Jesus, the Head of the Church, and those who gather to worship as members of his Body, becomes visible in the place of the Church where the Eucharist and other sacraments are celebrated.

Churches are pre-eminently there to provide worthy places, dedicated, consecrated, for the celebration of the liturgy. But being there they find a more varied use in our lives as a community of faith and as individuals.

Whenever someone slips into the church to pray before the tabernacle, or when a traveller far from home finds the place where Mass is celebrated, or when a child is brought to the church for baptism, or when a body is received for the funeral Liturgy - these various actions impress on us the importance of the church where we members of the Church come to do these things. And our doing of these things invests with profound significance these churches where we gather in prayer and worship, places where the faith and life of the Church come together and are made visible.

Changes

5. The faith of the Church is unchanging, but it is rare that church buildings do not bear signs of change. Shifts in population sometimes mean churches need extending, sometimes that they can become surplus to need; developments in theology, in liturgical practice and piety, in architectural style have their impact too. It has always been thus. Many Roman Catholic churches in England and Wales are of relatively recent date, thus relatively little changed. But if we look to the former Catholic churches of England - the medieval parish churches of England and Wales – we see in them many signs of change and development.

6. We see how single-cell Roman churches gave way to the two-cell constructions of the Anglo-Saxons, some in stone, some in wood. Almost all of these were replaced or substantially refashioned in a deliberate policy of political and religious conquest by the Normans. Subsequent generations perfected their building and engineering skills to the glory of God, creating great cathedrals and parish churches, sometimes working on new buildings but sometimes renovating older ones. The Reformation saw dramatic changes in church furnishings, with stone altars replaced by wooden tables, and statues, stained glass and screens destroyed or sold.

Few Catholic churches in regular use in England and Wales are more than 200 years old. The many churches built in the 19th and 20th Centuries bear witness to the growth and development of the Catholic community in England and Wales during this time, particularly in urban centres as the Church welcomed waves of immigrants and workers in industry. These churches too often bear the marks of change, the consequence of shifts in population and changes in liturgical practice and piety, especially of the liturgical reforms which followed on from the Second Vatican Council (1963-1965).

7. The renewal of the Liturgy mandated by the Second Vatican Council was inspired by one visionary theme: that under divine grace the Church is created and sustained by its liturgical life. The Church assembles at the font to enact its birth in the person of new members. It is gathered and schooled by the Word proclaimed at the ambo in its midst. It centres its life on the altar where the Eucharist, the source and summit of all its activity, is offered. The sacred space of a church building is given shape by the rites of the Church.

Each parish has a responsibility for the proper and dignified celebration of all these rites, therefore parishes will reflect from time to time on how best to employ the ritual space they have. Communities worshipping in older churches, particularly those which are listed, need to weigh carefully the requirements of a renewed Liturgy and the need to respect the historic and artistic values of the existing building. Those presented with the opportunity to build a new church should in turn accept the responsibility of creating an inheritance of value.

8. The Second Vatican Council's Constitution on the Sacred Liturgy, *Sacrosanctum Concilium*, published in 1963, called for the 'full, conscious and active participation' of the people to be the aim considered 'before all else' in the restoration of the Liturgy (SC 14). To this end the Church has authorised revision of the rites themselves so that they may convey more clearly what they signify, the translation of the texts into vernacular languages so the faithful may understand better the prayer of the Church. In addition, with respect to church buildings, many changes to fabric and layout have been made, to give the assembly a better view of the liturgical action, and particularly to more easily associate themselves with the action that is performed not by the presiding priest alone, but by the whole Christ, Body and Head (*Catechism of the Catholic Church* (CCC) 1136).

9. As the Church continues to reflect on the participation of its members in the Liturgy, it will want its buildings to be in concert with this overarching aim. It is true that older buildings may have been conceived and constructed with a vision of worship different from ours. That does not mean that they cannot continue in use, still less that change should be imposed regardless of the consequences. In the management of change to our buildings, historical and liturgical awareness are called to act in partnership with the creative and subtle design processes to ensure that necessary adaptations to our historic building inheritance respect equally the character of contemporary Liturgy and the historic or artistic merits of the church.

10. In the forty or so years since the liturgical reforms of the Second Vatican Council the introduction of the revised rites has had a profound effect on how the Liturgy is celebrated and understood. The principal focus, the heart of a church, remains the altar on which the Eucharist is celebrated, and the ambo from which the word is proclaimed. But around these, and ordered to them, there are other ritual spaces: for the rites of initiation, penance and reconciliation, marriage and holy orders. Within the church building space needs to be provided for the whole Liturgy to be celebrated with dignity by the gathered people of God.

11. Often the changes made immediately after the Council were intended especially to give the congregation a better view of the sanctuary and the actions that take place there. Subsequent experience has taught that this is not enough. Participation in the Liturgy calls for action and movement, not just by those on the sanctuary but by the whole assembly.

The Liturgy happens not just within the sanctuary but throughout the whole sacred space. In order to do the actions that are proper to it, the assembly needs to face in different directions, to process, to kneel and stand in comfort, the better to express its active role as the worshipping Body of Christ.

12. Church buildings have to facilitate many liturgical and devotional activities in addition to the celebration of Mass: celebration of the Sacrament of Penance, walking the Way of the Cross, meditation before the Blessed Sacrament and so on. They have to accommodate many different people as well. In the quest to provide an inclusive and hospitable place, access to all parts of the building should be equally available to all. As an instance of this, particular focus in recent years has been on legal changes favouring access for those with disabilities. The vocation of the community is to announce the Gospel to everyone and this has to be expressed not only in what the Church does but also in the buildings it uses.

13. This Directory seeks to clarify what is asked of communities by the teaching and worship of the Church after Vatican II. It offers guidance concerning the requirements made by the liturgical rites, and how these might best be responded to in existing churches and inform the building of those still to be constructed.

Liturgical Law

14. The Liturgy is an enacted statement of belief. The Church, therefore, exercises care for the integrity of her liturgical rites and how they are celebrated. One of the ways in which this is done is through liturgical law.

15. Liturgical law is enshrined in a variety of documents and it is important to appreciate the relative weight of the types of legislation. The interpretation of law is a complex area and the following is offered as a brief overview.

The liturgical law of the Church is given in a variety of different documents:

- Conciliar, most recently those of the Second Vatican Council;
- Papal;
- Curial, in the field of Liturgy particularly those of the Congregation for Divine Worship and the Discipline of the Sacraments;
- Local, originating from a diocesan bishop or from the Bishops' Conference.

The documents will either be:

- Theological (Examples include the Constitution on the Sacred Liturgy, SC);
- Legislative (Examples include the Code of Canon Law, the liturgical rites and their introductions) or
- Executive (Examples include Instructions issued by the Congregation for Divine Worship and the Discipline of the Sacraments, such as *Redemptionis Sacramentum* (RS) and this book issued by the Bishops' Conference of England and Wales. These seek to clarify the law and recommend an approach to be followed in implementing it).

16. Documents such as the *General Instruction of the Roman Missal* (GIRM) are legislative documents with force of law and their requirements should be observed. However the Church's liturgical laws, which apply to the construction and alteration of church buildings, are usually contained in the preamble to the liturgical books of the Roman Rite. The style of such legislation is usually less prescriptive than Canon Law, relying more on principles and guidance.

Civil Law

17. The right to religious freedom includes the right to freedom of worship, and this has implications for the care of buildings built for such worship. On its part, the Second Vatican Council and directives of the Holy See have reminded bishops of their need to exercise vigilance over the remodelling of places of worship and to protect works of art and sacred furnishings. It is the right and duty of the Ordinary to supervise the administration of temporal goods within his jurisdiction and the duty of Trustees to protect trust property vested in them. At the same time it is recognised that there will be a certain overlap between the concerns of the Church for her properties and the concern of civil authorities for the good management of land and properties in general as well as a responsibility to the common good of society.

18. The Church will therefore take fully into account the requirements of Civil Law as it applies to the work of church building and restoration. When the intention is to build a new church or extend an existing building planning permission and engagement with the local planning authority is of course required. In respect of those buildings which have been 'listed' as buildings of historic or architectural interest, the Church has secured the government's agreement to continue its role as the steward of its built inheritance under the system known as the Ecclesiastical Exemption. The requirements of Civil law concerning listed churches established in the 'Ecclesiastical Exemption (Listed Buildings and Conservation Areas) Order 1994' have been incorporated into Church law by means of Diocesan Statutes.

19. The term 'Exemption' does not mean that the Church is exempt from any control but means rather that in the case of listed churches and chapels which are in use as places of worship the State allows for statutory regulation of alterations not by the local authority's planning department but through the system of controls set out in the *Directory on the Ecclesiastical Exemption* issued by the Bishops' Conference of England and Wales. Under the Exemption scheme each diocese or group of dioceses (where appropriate) set up a body known as the Historic Churches Committee.

An outline of the procedure for work to listed churches is given in Part Two.

Part One

House of God, House of the people of God

20. *Lord,*
you built a holy Church,
founded upon the apostles
with Jesus Christ as its cornerstone.

Grant that your people, gathered in your name,
may fear and love you
and grow as the temple of your glory.

Collect, RDC, 17

21. *Lord, fill this place with your presence,*
and extend your hand
to all who call upon you.
May your word here proclaimed
and your sacraments here celebrated
strengthen the hearts of all the faithful.

Collect, RDC, 52

22. *May this building,*
which we dedicate to your name,
be a house of salvation and grace
where Christians gathered in fellowship
may worship you in spirit and truth
and grow together in love.

Concluding Prayer to the Litany, RDC, 60

What's in a name?

23. *'The term church means a sacred building intended for divine worship, to which the faithful have right of access for the exercise, especially the public exercise, of divine worship. (Code of Canon Law 1214)*

The building, the church, exists to serve the Church, the people of God. Our understanding of the meaning and purpose of the building must in great part be informed by our understanding of the meaning and purpose of the people. In the first place, the church is a house for the Church.

24. In this sense the Christian church stands in contradistinction to the temples and shrines of other religions. These were seen to be the house of God, or of a god. Thus commonly in the ancient world when people, Jews or pagans, offered worship at a Temple they did so from outside, the interior of the Temple being reserved to the gods, or in the case of Jerusalem's Temple, to the God of Israel.

25. *Come to him, a living stone, though rejected by mortals yet chosen and precious in God's sight, and like living stones, let yourselves be built into a spiritual house, to be a holy priesthood, to offer spiritual sacrifices acceptable to God through Jesus Christ.*

1 Peter 2:4-5, *NRSV*

However the witness of the New Testament is that the Christian Temple is not so much a building of stone, as a building of living stones. The Christian Temple is the Christian people built on the foundation of Christ, the living cornerstone.

26. *You are no longer strangers and aliens, but you are citizens with the saints and also members of the household of God, built upon the foundation of the apostles and prophets, with Christ Jesus himself as the cornerstone. In him the whole structure is joined together and grows into a holy temple in the Lord; in whom you also are built together spiritually into a dwelling place for God.*

Ephesians 2:19-22, *NRSV*

Paul in Ephesians sees the Christian community itself as being a holy temple, a dwelling place of God, but it became commonplace to speak of where the church gathered, the house of the Church, (*domus ecclesiae*) as being also the house of God (*domus Dei*). It is important to recognise that both of these understandings have found a firm place in the Catholic Christian tradition. Both inform the *Rite of Dedication of a Church*, and both need to be respected in contemporary use and design of churches.

27. In the New Testament the Greek noun *ekklesia* is used first of the community, called together into solemn assembly by the Lord. Only later is it applied to the community's place of worship. This Greek word finds its way into English, via its Latin transliteration, and is found in such uses as 'ecclesiastical.' It is also the origin of the Welsh word *eglwys* ('church'). It is worth noting that *ekklesia* is also a synonym of the Greek *sunagoge*, which transliterated gives our English word 'synagogue', the word still used by many Jews to name their assemblies and their places of worship.

The English words 'Church' and 'church' have a different derivation. They come from the Greek noun *kuriake* (that which belongs to the Lord). In this case *kuriake* seems first to have been applied to the building rather than to the people. It finds its way into English via the Old English form *kirike*. *Kuriake* is also the origin of the Scots word 'kirk'.

A place for worship

28. The pre-eminent purpose of these buildings of the Church is to provide a place for the people to gather to celebrate the Liturgy, the source and summit of Christian life. The buildings also have a secondary but honoured purpose, which comes into its own especially when the community of faith is not gathered in solemn assembly. For then the building itself remains, not an empty shell, but serving as a physical reminder of the abiding presence of God amongst his people. This building is not only the place where the community gathers for worship, but where in its gathering and its worship the community encounters the risen Lord of Life. A house for the Church, a house for God: from the earliest times in the Church's history the community has taken care to ensure its churches are equal to meeting both purposes to the full.

A tension between adoration and participation

29. The normal practice in Christianity has been for a particular community to be linked with a particular church – the place where the members of that community gather for their weekly, even their daily prayer. However, in addition to its parish churches and cathedrals, the Church has from the earliest times, certainly from the 3rd Century, built other buildings to contain other acts of worship. Perhaps most notable are those built to house the relics of a saint or to 'contain' a particular place, held to be holy because it has been the place at which the divine has been made manifest. Examples include the basilica of St Peter's in Rome built to provide a church for those coming to worship at the tomb of Peter, the First of the Apostles, and the 4th Century basilicas of the Holy Land: Bethlehem, built to mark the places of, for example, Christ's birth, and his death and resurrection.

30. Within these churches the 'shrine' proper was separated in some way from the area set aside for 'regular' liturgical worship. Thus in Bethlehem the holy grotto is underneath the church in a crypt; in Jerusalem the place for celebration of the Eucharist was in a basilica separate from the place of the Cross or the tomb of Christ. This practice was continued in later centuries too: thus in churches built on the pilgrimage route to Compostela relics were reserved in a place separate from the central parts of the church where the Liturgy was celebrated. Pilgrims accessed the relics by way of an ambulatory and thus their devotion guarded from compromising the place of the Liturgy proper.

31. In the Roman Catholic Church changes in the modes of liturgical celebration meant that making such a clear separation between the holy place or the holy object and the place of 'regular' liturgical worship became much more difficult. Places of reservation came to exert a more pervasive influence over the ordering of the whole liturgical space. However this influence came not from the reservation of relics of saints or holy sites, but from a new concern for the reservation of the Blessed Sacrament.

32. A variety of factors, including the Eucharistic controversies of the 9th Century onwards, led to changes in how congregations participated in the celebration of the Mass. Rather than their participation finding its natural culmination in the reception of Holy Communion, lay participation was more commonly achieved through the actions of watching and adoration. This shift found its complement in a new emphasis on the reservation of the Blessed Sacrament outside of Mass, on providing a place for the reservation worthy of the Sacrament and suitable for private and public acts of adoration.

33. Previously the Blessed Sacrament had been reserved discretely for the purposes of Viaticum. Now the place of reservation tended to become the focus of the building as a whole, dominating it, during the celebration of the Liturgy as well as outside of it. The sanctuary was set apart from the rest of the Church as much by virtue of its being the place of reservation of the sacred host as of its being the place for the action of offering the sacrifice of the Mass.

Recent reforms

34. The recent reform of the Liturgy mandated by the Second Vatican Council has sought to restore a sense of priority to the action of the worshipping assembly as the first principle which should govern the ordering of a church. This is entirely without prejudice to the significance of the reserved sacrament, and indeed in those churches where reordering has been particularly successful, the particular honour paid to the Blessed Sacrament is all the more clear because of the care paid to the provision and decoration of the place of reservation.

35. Whichever understanding is most fully expressed in any particular building – whether this place is considered as first the House of the Church or the House of God (*domus ecclesiae* or *domus Dei*) – what must never be lost sight of is that this place exists for the people. It is here to assist those who gather here to grow in faith, to live in faith and to progress from this world, where the Church has no permanent home, to the promised New Jerusalem, where there will be no Temple, but where all will be gathered before the Lamb.

Witnesses in stone

36. From the earliest times the Church has organised and decorated its places of worship to give rich witness to what it believes. Even before the Christian faith found expression in the written words of Scripture or of exhortation or theological reflection, it had found expression in the rich symbolism of the rituals that we know as sacraments. In time these rituals were contained, framed, accompanied and enabled through the careful and inspired use of architecture and other liturgical arts. Buildings and their decoration proved themselves apt to bearing profound witness to the faith of the Church.

37. If we take the example of one of the earliest known church buildings, that of Dura-Europus in present day Syria, we see how in the middle of the 3rd Century the community of Dura-Europus gave expression to its faith by the decisions they made about the way they worshipped and how they 'housed' that worship. It was important to them that the whole Church should be able to gather together each week to share in the food of Word and Eucharist. But their building did not enable this, the rooms were too small. So they adapted it, knocking down walls to provide themselves with a large enough gathering space for the celebration of the Eucharist. They also knew the particular significance of baptism, by which the Church made Christians, and bore witness to its importance and dignity by reserving a special room for the celebration of this sacrament, and affording it the richest decoration of all the rooms used by the Church.

38. And so it has been down through the centuries. Christian artists and designers have been called on to design and fashion spaces suited to the Church's worship, and to decorate and elaborate these spaces all the better to represent the mysteries of faith celebrated there.

Enrichment through the arts

39. *In order to communicate the message entrusted to her by Christ, the Church needs art. Art must make perceptible, and as far as possible attractive, the world of the spirit, of the invisible, of God. It must therefore translate into meaningful terms that which is in itself ineffable. ...The Church needs architects, because she needs spaces to bring the Christian people together and celebrate the mysteries of salvation. After the terrible destruction of the last World War and the growth of great cities, a new generation of architects showed themselves adept at responding to the exigencies of Christian worship, confirming that the religious theme can still inspire architectural design in our own day. Not infrequently these architects have constructed churches which are both places of prayer and true works of art.*

Letter of Pope John Paul II to Artists, 12.

40. *So that the splendour of worship will shine out through the fittingness of beauty of liturgical art...it will be appropriate to make provision for projects to train the craftsmen and artists who are commissioned to build and decorate places destined for liturgical use. At the root of the guidelines (offered in* Sacrosanctum Concilium *122) is a vision of art, and of sacred art in particular, that relates it to the 'infinite beauty of God in works made by human hands'.*

Letter of Pope John Paul II, *Spiritus et Sponsa* (SS)
On the 40th Anniversary of Sacrosanctum Concilium 5.

41. The patrimony of the Church is rich in places designed for gathering and worship – the ancient house churches and basilicas of Rome; the Gothic Cathedrals and Abbeys of England and France; country parish churches; chapels and basilicas.

42. These places for worship are frequently enriched by their contents:

- crafted objects which directly serve the liturgical rites e.g. the altar, ambo, font, vessels, vestments and books;
- the decoration that elaborates and decorates the place of worship e.g. the decoration of doors, walls and floors, the design and decoration of windows;
- the images that serve devotion e.g. images of Christ, our Lady, the Saints; Stations of the Cross.

Such churches and their buildings are among the high points of cultural and artistic achievement in Western Europe. They are treasures not only of and for the Church, but for all humankind.

43. Sacred buildings and works of sacred art can reach across the divide between the sacred and the secular. For those who use them for their primary intended purpose they shape and enrich ritual and prayer. But the artistic patrimony of the Church can witness something of the mystery of faith even to those who do not profess faith in God or in the saving death and resurrection of Jesus. Often they bear eloquent witness to Christian faith and values in ways that beggar our verbal preaching and teaching.

44. It is a mistake to think that such artistic creativity is a thing of the past. In the past 100 years, in our own land, there have been enormous contributions to the church's rich patrimony of buildings and liturgical arts. Many are the exceptional works of modern and contemporary art which nourish our lives of faith.

45. The range of these various works, ancient and modern, is immense. Each is the result of an artist's creative response to what is revealed in the history of salvation, and to what the Church does in her celebration of the mysteries of salvation - making fullest use of the creativity gifted them by God to produce a new work of art. Each work, a fresh 'naming' of that which is of God; under the inspiration of the Spirit, each work a means by which artists witness to the glory, truth and beauty of God.

Contemporary responsibilities

46. Those charged with care of our Liturgy and our churches today have the responsibility of seeking to draw on the creativity of men and women in our own age, to ensure that our places of worship continue to be enriched by the work of artists and designers.

47. Such work should respond creatively both to contemporary culture and be respectful of the artistic and design values already explicit in many of our churches. Also, it must have the ability to speak appropriately of the Mystery of the Catholic Faith.

A place of prayer

48. In accordance with the teaching of Second Vatican Council the Church's priority must be to ensure that a church truly comes into its own when the community gathers there, when the articulation of space in that place enables the articulation and celebration of faith. If a church does not do that it fails in its principal purpose.

49. However even when the church is empty, it is most desirable that it continue to function as a place capable of prompting and enabling prayer, feeding it and forming it. The Eastern Christian tradition especially emphasises the cosmic dimension of their churches, understanding them to be places where heaven is at home on earth, and earth raised up to the heavens. Western Catholics find the quiet of an 'empty' church conducive to prayer as they respond to the presence of the Lord in the reserved Sacrament, fruit of our worship in him. Care about the design and ordering and decoration of churches can ensure that something of the transcendent is there even when the Liturgy is not being celebrated.

50. The primary liturgical fittings – the altar, the ambo, the presider's chair and the font – will perhaps prompt prayer in thanksgiving for the good gifts we receive there in Christ.

51. Western Catholics, in particular, often find particular focus and assistance for their prayer provided by statues in the church, reminding us of the communion of saints, encouraging us to turn to them in prayer, seeking their encouragement and intercession. Other traditions make use of icons, in a related way, although underpinned by a different theology of image.

52. There is much even in an 'empty church' that can help people to pray and pray well. In our busy world of today the mere opportunity to be in an 'empty' place, a place of refuge, of peace and quiet, provides a chance to relax and seek to make sense of our daily lives in a building redolent of the eternity of God (*cf. Celebrating the Mass* (CTM) 96).

53. There are many of our contemporaries who have never entered a church. Yet they will be familiar with the exterior of our buildings – even the little that they see can serve as a reminder of the Lord they do not know, or perhaps know only in small part, and of the community of the Church. Church buildings offer a reminder of the Church's presence in an area, and make concrete the abstractions of Church and Faith. They offer a tacit invitation to those who live near them to come and see: this is where the Church is; look at us and see how we live; talk with us and learn why we live this way.

54. The value of such witness provided by church buildings to a secular world should not be underestimated. Again and again at times of crisis we see how readily the local community will turn to its churches as places to gather for prayer and reflection. It is to be hoped that as they enter in they find them welcoming, and places which affirm the gospel message of God's love and care of his people.

55. Of course we take a risk when we let people know who and where we are – maybe they will demand more of us than we will find it easy to give. But this is what the mission of the Church invites us to say 'yes' to.

Part Two

PROCESS

56. *May this work begin, continue,*
and be brought to fulfilment in Christ,
for he is Lord for ever and ever.

From the Prayer of Blessing of a Church's foundation stone, RDC, 27.

57. When the Church of Dura-Europus realised that it had became too large for the room in which it was meeting and knocked down a dividing wall to give itself more space, it established a pattern that has been followed countless times since. Church buildings are changed and developed in response to the changing circumstances, needs and expectations of the worshipping community. Sometimes these changes have been prompted by theological, liturgical or architectural developments. Sometimes they have been prompted by political, social, demographic, cultural or legal developments.

58. These same factors are among those which influence the Church of today, causing communities to consider building a new church, or reordering an existing one. Some of these factors may come from new experiences within the community itself - for example, growing experience of adult initiation can lead to a new concern and care for how the sacrament of baptism, in particular, might best be celebrated to reveal its meaning and significance. Others might be more the result of external factors, such as a local programme of house building moving people into an area, or the closure of local industries moving people away from it. Another example of this has been the way that the raising of consciousness and the passing of legislation has encouraged parishes to look more carefully at the obstacles their buildings might place in the way of disabled people and how these might be overcome.

Change and development

59. Change can be a welcome experience for some and a threatening one for others. The prospect of any change to our parish churches provides a fertile environment for both reactions; tensions will arise no matter how carefully the whole community is involved in the process. Our buildings provide settings for significant moments in peoples' lives and the memories attached to them, so it is often a painful process to change something, even when all the reasons are understood.

60. All processes of catechesis and consultation should ensure that every voice is heard, and diocesan and other procedures need to be followed carefully. The community is encouraged to understand that it is part of a living tradition which has made changes throughout history, and that each generation will add to and take away from its own places of worship.

Who might be involved?

61. The work of considering change to a church is not a matter for any one person or any particular group. It should always be a collaborative process involving the various parties with interest and/or responsibility for the Church and its buildings.

The parish

62. The parish priest has particular responsibility for the parish and its property. He should ensure that the parish community has every opportunity to consider and comment on proposed changes at every stage – from identifying current needs through to assessment of final designs and beyond. Commonly such consultation will need to be integrated with formation of the parish community concerning the Church's authentic teaching on the liturgy and church ordering.

The diocese

63. The parish priest ministers in communion, and under the authority of, the bishop of the diocese. Diocesan procedures for the approval of change and for the incurring of expenditure must be observed at all times.

64. The various bodies who are likely to be involved in considering proposals include:

- the Diocesan Liturgy Commission and its Art and Architecture Committee;
- the Diocesan Property Service agency;
- the Historic Churches Committee (this Committee will always involved in considering and approving proposals concerning listed buildings, but its expertise is also available to be called on where non-listed buildings, or their contents, are of particular significance for the patrimony of the Church);
- the Diocesan Trustees.

65. Whether a reordering of an existing church or the building of a new church is being considered there should be early involvement of the responsible diocesan authorities for example, the diocesan Art and Architecture Committee, Liturgy Commission, Property Services or Finance Office. A church which is listed will always be subject to the Historic Churches procedure.

Specialists

66. As part of the responsibility for its buildings the parish will, in all but the most minor projects, need to engage with specialists. This may involve architects and artists, those with special qualifications in the conservation of historic churches as well as experts in sound, lighting, heating and energy efficiency.

The wider community

67. As has already been noted, (see 17–19, 53–55 above) churches are of significance to more than the Church. The importance of consultation with other interested parties is already an important part of the legislation governing the operation of Historic Churches Committees. Public consultation is also something that should be considered in the case of changes and developments concerning other churches, particularly where those changes will directly impact on others, individuals or groups. (See especially 85 below)

Starting points

68. The desire to make changes to an existing church building or build a new church can arise through reflection on three different things: the liturgy, the building and the community. As a rule, changes ought to be made in response to need. The initial perception of need requires careful assessment and refinement and may lead in directions that were not part of the first consideration. It can help at the beginning of the process to prepare a formal 'statement of need' as a starting point for those involved in the project.

69. The need may be liturgical:

- there is no space at the entrance to the church for baptismal, wedding and funeral parties to be welcomed;
- steps or other barriers impede or even prevent wheelchair and pushchair access to parts of the liturgical/worship space;
- steps or other barriers make it difficult to distribute Holy Communion under both species in an orderly and reverent way;
- fixed seating alongside aisles blocks the communion procession when there is a coffin in place;
- a choir or music group is established or moves to sing in a new place, or an organ is moved or replaced;
- a 'temporary' altar needs to be replaced by a fixed one.

70. A starting point may be the building. There will be cases where past reorderings need serious reconsideration from either a liturgical or aesthetic point of view, or indeed from both. In the course of such a reconsideration it may be seen that lost or removed historical or aesthetic features can be restored or reinstated. If such restoration is judged likely to enhance the celebration of the Liturgy or assist devotion, then this is desirable. The regular Quinquennial report may indicate the need for some conservation, repairs or structural alteration to meet legal requirements, e.g. provision for the needs of people with disabilities.

71. The need for change may arise from changes within the community itself: changes in local demographics or a renewed vision of the role of the parish within the wider community. Parishes seeking to make changes to their church must reflect upon their internal character as worshipping communities (i.e. as local communities but within the community of the Church), while remembering too their outward nature as communities of witness to Christ in the secular world. There should also be cognisance of and engagement with current secular conservation procedures and philosophy, especially in regard to listed buildings and buildings in conservation areas.

72. It was noted in the Introduction (8–11) that the various parts of the church are interdependent. Changes to the altar may have implications with regard to the ambo, which may have an effect on seating, which may, in turn, reveal a need to reconsider the lighting of the church. In a similar way matters to do with the building may have implications for how the liturgy is celebrated.

73. Sometimes a project that has its origins in a consideration of something that seems rather simple and straightforward will, when time is given for proper reflection, turn out to have much deeper implications. A project that might have first been thought of as a simple reordering might end up actually requiring a major rebuilding of the church. The opposite, of course, might also be the case.

Considering the ordering of an existing church

74. Once the possibility of change to an existing church is being seriously discussed questions such as these are likely to start to arise:

- What will it cost? what can we afford?
- Where will the altar/ambo/tabernacle etc. be placed?
- Can we make continued use of artefacts from the older building?
- What provision is to be made for Baptism?
- How do we understand terms such as 'worthy' and 'of good quality'?
- Has our church got or might it receive listed building status?
- Where can we go for help and advice?
- How do we work with an architect?
- What other changes might be identified?
- How do we prioritise?
- How can we involve as many of the community as possible in the process?

75. These are good questions to ask, and deserve answers. Changes in church buildings involve a large commitment: in money, in time, in people's faith and emotional involvement and their vision of themselves as the Church. A parish needs to do all it can to ensure that it comes up with good answers to perceived problems – otherwise there will be confusion and disappointment.

76. The process of making a decision will inevitably require a community to ask big questions in order to make sure that its answers are adequate. It will need to look critically at its liturgical celebration but also to the quality of its Christian life and witness.

77. It is for that reason that it is recommended that when a parish is beginning to engage with anything but the most minor of changes, it should engage in a process of thorough review of how the Liturgy is presently celebrated. This will help to involve the whole parish community and enable all concerned to understand more fully the Liturgy and its intended role in the life of the community. Such a process involves looking at what the Liturgy is, how the Church expects it to be celebrated, and why it has these expectations. Assistance with such a review process can be obtained from Diocesan Liturgy Commissions and the Liturgy Office of the Bishops' Conference.

78. Good catechesis using the appropriate church documents, reflections on parish practice, perhaps videos of real celebrations and the memories of older parishioners, will help both the working group and the community as a whole to have a clearer understanding of what the official Church teaches and how that may be interpreted. It also renews the vision of every person as a member of the Body of Christ, called to worship in this place, each with a valued part to play. From this may arise a new layer of questions, such as:

- What should be the style, shape, size, setting of the liturgical space(s)?
- How can the relationship between the various sacraments and other liturgies be indicated by the ordering of the various liturgical spaces?
- How can the setting for reconciliation express the healing and reintegration with the Church it accomplishes, while also providing appropriate security for priest and people?
- How can the various ministers be seen to be part of the assembly?
- Does the space inspire participation, or passive observation?
- Where can people pray quietly? What are our local devotions?
- What will happen to the items that are no longer needed, but which people feel strongly about?
- How can access be provided for all? Will there be parking? A processional way?
- How will we celebrate the Easter Triduum?
- Why a new church, when it will cost so much?
- Why change when we are so attached to what is already there?
- How can we identify and use important historic fabric and artefacts?

79. These questions are not in any order of significance, or in a particularly logical sequence; they may not even all arise. However they do represent a fairly random selection of questions which come from a deeper understanding of what happens when the church meets for worship, and put the question into the wider context of the mission of the Church in the world. Catechesis and consultation with the parish community are vital parts of the process.

80. Such a process will inform the parish's self understanding, and provide invaluable for the group coordinating the reordering process. It will take time. Exploring the various issues may involve the parish trying out temporary arrangements and reflecting on them over weeks or months. As has already been clear such a process extends beyond mere questions of how to arrange the liturgical furnishing, and should encourage the community to examine its various activities and understand them as part of the mission of the Church. Again, this will take time, and it will require a commitment to the process on the part of the parish leadership. However, as a result of such commitment the eventual outcome is more likely to be a clearer and more helpful self understanding on the part of the parish, a better brief for the architect and in the longer term bring about a healthier parish, more committed to and better able for a committed living out of its faith.

Building a new church: considerations and decisions

81. Reasons for building a new church may include factors such as:

- *major shifts in local population:* the church has become too large or small for the present and forecast needs of the community. Or it may be that local redevelopment and its effects – new houses, schools, shops, roads, industry - mean that the building is now in the wrong place for the people;
- *changes in organisation of the Church locally:* amalgamation or clustering of parishes might invite the building of a new church to serve this community;
- *good use of resources and careful stewardship:* in some cases it may cost more to restore a church in very poor repair, without necessarily providing a dignified and suitable place for the celebration of the Liturgy by the whole assembly, than to build a new church;
- *evangelisation and witness:* a church is a sign to the world of the presence of Jesus Christ among his people, a lively and prayerful centre of the activity of the church, where its members come and go for nourishing and mission. Where new churches are built those responsible for their design and building should seek to engage with contemporary architectural styles as creatively and as fruitfully as did previous generations.

82. Where building a new church is a possibility the issues raised in paragraphs 74–80 will also need to be considered. It may only be by going through such a process that the possibility is looked at.

Buildings no longer used for worship

83. When the building of a new church will impact on the future of an existing church this matter must be afforded careful consideration. It might for example raise questions about the old church building, its contents, furnishings, liturgical and devotional sites.

84. As soon as it is considered that any particular church or chapel may be surplus to the needs of the Church, great care must be taken with consultation and decision making. Competent advice should always be sought regarding any issue of disposal, relocation and reuse. Failure to comply with agreed procedures, and not only in the case of listed buildings and prominent buildings in conservation areas, can easily provoke controversy at national level which can have a negative impact on the Church.

85. It should be a matter of concern to the community to avoid the controversy that can be generated locally by proposed change involving a well-known local landmark. Potential difficulties can often be avoided if full and effective consultation with all stakeholders is carried out at an early stage. It is essential that when any such change is being considered those involved should be aware of the legitimate concerns of the secular authorities, all interested parties, and an understanding of current conservation policy and practice are essential in such circumstances. The Historic Churches Committee and the Patrimony Committee of the Bishops' Conference can assist in offering advice.

86. It is a specific requirement of the Ecclesiastical Exemption Scheme that in all cases where it is proposed to close a listed church or chapel the Historic Churches Committee is to commission a report on the building and its contents. Both this report and the wider consultation should inform the decision making process. The details of what needs to be done in this regard are set out in the Bishops' Conference Directory on Ecclesiastical Exemption.

Keeping a balance

87. No two churches are the same. No two parish communities are alike. No two celebrations are identical. There is no 'approved' plan for a new church, no single solution to a church reordering, no blueprint which will fit every parish. Within any project there are three aspects to consider: the Liturgy, the people and the building. In any decision made as part of the process these three must be held in balance:

- *the Liturgy* – the requirements set out in liturgical law (in the Introductions to the Rites) for the reverent and graceful celebration of the rites themselves; how the rites are celebrated in the parish; devotional practices;
- *the people* – the composition of the community: families, elderly people, commuters, tourists; where they live, their employment, their income and interests; their understanding of themselves as Church;
- *the building* – its value as a symbol and sign to the Christian community and wider community; its architectural and historical significance; its function as a shelter for the gathered community.

Added to these are external factors: finance; the legal requirements concerning health and safety, access for people with disabilities, conservation and planning; whether a building is listed or in a conservation area; architectural and heritage considerations.

88. *No single aspect should dominate the whole process.* A new church or a reordering driven by liturgical principles, ignoring the pastoral needs of the community and the historic value of the building is as wrong as an aesthetic/historic restoration which disregards liturgical norms, or a community project that neglects the primary function of the church in favour of multiple uses.

89. However good the work, though, it will not on its own improve the liturgical celebration of a parish; what is needed is prayer, catechesis and formation, leadership and the guidance of the Holy Spirit.

Working with the diocese

90. Although each diocese will differ somewhat in detail, it is generally the case that the *Liturgy Commission* and the *Art and Architecture Committee* is responsible to the Bishop for evaluating projects for liturgical reordering or new building proposed by parishes. These bodies will assess the liturgical, artistic and architectural suitability of a project and make appropriate recommendations to the Bishop.

91. The diocesan committees will also be able to offer advice and consultancy services to parishes on the Liturgy review process, compilation of a design brief and selection of an architect, artist and other specialists. It is helpful to all concerned if parishes obtain such advice before they begin the formal processes of seeking approval for projects: it can help avoid any problems later on.

92. In the case of all but the most insignificant changes to the liturgical arrangements or appearance of a church, the diocesan committees will require plans of the existing building and detailed plans and drawings of what is proposed together with details of materials etc., in order properly to evaluate the project in question. While photographs of the church are useful, a site visit will usually be necessary.

93. Where any changes at all are being proposed to a listed building these changes need to be referred to the *Historic Churches Committee*. As a statutory body the Historic Churches Committee has the role of ensuring that any changes, liturgical or otherwise, made to any listed church are made in a manner respectful of that church's historical and architectural significance and consonant with the wider public good. The Historic Churches Committee will, after proper consultation and consideration, advise the Bishop to issue or withhold the faculty necessary for the work to proceed.

94. When a church, although unlisted, is of particular architectural or artistic merit, or lies within a designated conservation area, the Historic Churches Committee may be consulted as a source of specialist advice. The possibility of spot-listing should also be born in mind, namely whether a presently unlisted church might persuasively be argued for as appropriate for listing. The same care should be taken over such buildings as is afforded to listed churches.

95. Formal submissions to the Historic Churches Committee concerning works on a listed building may only be made after prior approval has been gained from the diocesan Liturgy Commission and Art and Architecture Committee or other diocesan body if the works proposed do not relate to the Liturgy. The diocesan Finance and Property authority will also have given its prior approval.

96. Once a proposal has been accepted subject to approval by the Historic Churches Committee it is then to be formally submitted to the Historic Churches Committee for its consideration. The Historic Churches Committee will advise the Bishop to issue or to withhold a faculty for such works. Work on listed churches and chapels may only be undertaken once such a faculty has been granted.

97. Although there is a proper sequence for formal approval of works, Historic Churches Committees and other Diocesan bodies work collaboratively. It is common practice for both the client and other Diocesan bodies to consult with the Historic Churches Committee prior to formal submissions being made. Such early consultation with the Historic Churches Committee is highly desirable to avoid delay and disappointment. It is advisable for consultation to take place well before a detailed scheme is drawn up in order to avoid abortive work and thus expense.

98. Under the Exemption Scheme, the Historic Churches Committee will consult with the statutory authorities prior to determining any application. Government policy on the protection and conservation of historic buildings is set out in an official document, namely Planning Policy Guidance note 15 (PPG 15). Planning Policy Guidance note 16 (PPG 16) deals with archaeology and the need for recording prior to changes taking place. It needs to be remembered that archaeological considerations apply to above ground structures as well as to remains below ground. The Patrimony Committee of the Bishops' Conference has drawn up a list of other publications that will assist and has issued Guidance Notes on various aspects of work to churches. They can be accessed on the Patrimony Committee's webpages, http://www.catholic-ew.org.uk/liturgy/Department/Patrimony.html

Working with specialists

99. Building a new church or reordering an existing one will of necessity involve a variety of people with specialist and professional skills. Some will be readily available, others less so. Making proper use of such people will mean that projects do not fail in matters of detail. Reliable advice will also help to ensure the avoidance of needless costs. When specialist practitioners are engaged they should be given as full an overview of the whole project as is possible, so that they can see how their work will influence the whole project and its future maintenance.

100. Diocesan committees for Liturgy and art and architecture and the local Historic Churches Committee will normally have access to a wide range of specialists, both local and national. They will also be able to access people with appropriate experience and skill in managing church projects and working in church buildings. They will be able to offer advice and assistance with preparing briefing documents, work schedules and the like. Diocesan legal and property services will be able to help with the wording of contracts to avoid unnecessary costs and ensure the successful completion of works.

101. Of particular importance to any project will be the *architect* or *liturgical designer*. Parishes will choose somebody after seeking the advice of the Diocesan Liturgy Commission. Listed churches will require someone with suitable experience of working with historic buildings and the Historic Churches Committee will be able to offer advice.

Architects should generally have experience of Church work and a good understanding of the liturgical requirements. It may be helpful for members of the parish to visit previous work by the architect.

Architectural competitions

102. One way to investigate alternative designs for a new church building is to set up a competition. Architects are invited to submit a basic design and two or three are then invited to work up more detailed plans (for which a small payment is made). A detailed brief, including a good overview of the parish community, is essential. A competition is a slow process, but it often brings innovative designs from younger architects. Before an appointment is made, it is essential to look at an architect's previous work and talk to the clients. Does the building fit their brief? What pleases them especially? Are there any drawbacks?

Practicalities

103. Before a turf is lifted, there are other questions which need to be addressed, for example:

- Will work in the church mean the building will be placed out of action for a period? If so will this affect Sunday Mass, or only weekday services? How much notice will the parish wish to give those planning weddings? What will be the implication for funerals?
- How and where will the reserved Blessed Sacrament and the holy oils be kept during this time?
- Will it be possible to maintain a quiet place for prayer somewhere on the site?
- Will it be necessary to store items (for example, benches, statues, vessels and altar supplies, repository goods, stained glass windows) during this period and if so, is there space on site or would specialist storage be preferable? Is this also a time to have repairs and maintenance work done on such items?
- How will the church or site be kept secure while work is in progress?
- Will the community's celebration of major feasts such as Christmas or Easter be affected? If so what alternative arrangements will need to be made? (The possibility of joining with another parish should not be discounted.)
- How will the community be kept informed of progress?

Caring for the heritage

104. Before any work is planned in detail, a number of procedures for the care and conservation of existing buildings or contents should be undertaken:

- An archive should be created (if none exists already) of drawings, photographs, plans and any other material relating to the history of the church. A search should be made of parish archives, diocesan records and records held by secular authorities, as well as material held by parishioners and other individuals, to create this archive.
- In all churches an inventory of all goods, articles and furnishings belonging to the church should be made and kept up-to-date. All pieces should be photographed individually and entered on a database. The provenance of objects and artefacts such as vestments, plate (chalices, ciboria, candlesticks, monstrances etc.), furnishings (altar, tabernacle, ambo etc.) and, where necessary, records of donors of such objects should be included. Detailed advice on making inventories is available from the Patrimony Committee of the Bishops' Conference.
- During the works themselves, a photographic record should be kept. This will enable features that are discovered during work to be recorded and decisions made as to how to deal with them.
- Disposal of items should only be done if absolutely necessary. This should be after consultation with the diocesan art and architecture committee, as well as the Bishop and the Historic Churches Committee as and when necessary. Consideration should be given to the feelings of donors or their heirs. An appropriate home, perhaps in another church or a museum or gallery, should be given to all articles so disposed of. Consideration should also be given to storage pending use in the future. In certain cases this may be insisted on by the relevant authority as a condition of any faculty granted. Chalices and vessels that hold the Blessed Sacrament must not be sold. (See Appendix C)
- Our church buildings are part of the heritage both of the universal Church and of communities of people living in particular places at particular times. When one generation hands on to the next, the tradition is rarely untouched but reflects the values and beliefs of those who have lived it. The task of this generation is to shape buildings out of our Catholic Christian tradition which will enable us to worship in integrity and faith and hand on to our children buildings which they will receive and then reshape to proclaim the message of the Good News to another age.

Planning ahead, looking to the future

105. If it becomes clear to a community that a major change is necessary, it may not always be possible for all the work to be done at once. It is best practice in every case to prepare a master plan which, subject to necessary approvals and faculty (if the church is listed), may then be carried out in phases within a reasonable period.

Marking the completion of works carried out by celebration of the Liturgy

106. The endpoint of a project will be marked by celebration. For example:

- The building of a new church, the substantial reordering or placing of a new altar in an existing church is marked by the celebration of the Rite of Dedication. Through the solemn celebration of the Eucharist the building is dedicated to God.
- New fixtures and fittings – such as an ambo, font, tabernacle or organ – are marked by the celebration of the appropriate Rite of Blessing.

A Mass of Thanksgiving may always be celebrated to mark the completion of any works carried out.

107. The *Rite of Dedication* needs careful preparation by the local community in liaison with the diocese.

Part Three

A Place for Celebration

Part One of this book has outlined the relationship between the Church which worships and the churches built to house the worship of the Church.

Part Two has explained the process to be considered when building a new church or when making changes to, reordering, an existing one.

Part Three deals with practical theology and its application. It takes areas and elements within the church in turn and gathers together the requirements and references in the various rites and documents of the Church. It sets out liturgical law and gives guidelines. This is the most practical section in the book.

The principles set out here do not provide a blueprint for every church but offer parameters within which those responsible for each church may safely work as they seek to enable their church to best serve the worship of the Church.

In this part of the book the various elements of a church are dealt with in separate sections. However, those concerned with the provision and ordering of sacred spaces need to think of each element in the light of the others, as all are related and form part of one single setting for the Sacred Liturgy.

Part Four of the book will outline the need for the continuing care of our church buildings in the light of their significance both as places of Catholic worship and as forming part of the patrimony of the wider community, both local and national.

1. A HOUSE FOR WORSHIP

108. *Here may your children,*
gathered around your altar,
celebrate the memorial of the Paschal Lamb,
and be fed at the table
of Christ's word and Christ's body.

Here may prayer, the Church's banquet,
resound through heaven and earth
as a plea for the world's salvation.

Here may the poor find justice,
the victims of oppression, true freedom.

From here may the whole world
clothed in the dignity of the children of God,
enter with gladness your city of peace.

Prayer of dedication, RDC, 62

109. *How lovely is your dwelling place, O Lord of hosts!*

Psalm 84

110. *For the celebration of the Eucharist, the People of God normally are gathered together in a church or, if there is no church or if it is too small, then in another respectable place that is nonetheless worthy of so great a mystery. Churches, therefore, and other places should be suitable for carrying out the sacred action and for ensuring the active participation of the faithful. Sacred buildings and requisites for divine worship should, moreover, be truly worthy and beautiful and be signs and symbols of heavenly realities.*

GIRM 288

111. *The People of God, gathered for Mass, has a coherent and hierarchical structure, which finds its expression in the variety of ministries and the variety of actions according to the different parts of the celebration. The general ordering of the sacred building must be such that in some way it conveys the image of the gathered assembly and allows the appropriate ordering of all the participants, as well as facilitating each in the proper carrying out of his function.*

The faithful and the choir should have a place that facilitates their active participation.

GIRM 294

112. *The space for the faithful is to be planned with special care, so as to enable them to take part properly in the sacred actions, with eyes and heart... Care should be taken that [they] are not only able to see the celebrant and other ministers, but that, with the help of modern amplifying systems, they are able to hear them easily also.*

Instruction *Inter Oecumenici*, 98

Principles

113. The church building is:

- where the Church celebrates the Liturgy, first and foremost the Sunday Eucharist, and the feast of Easter, both of these in their distinctive ways providing a foretaste of the Kingdom of God;
- where people gather to mark key moments in life: baptisms, weddings, funerals;
- the place where the Blessed Sacrament is reserved for the communion of those who are sick and for prayer and adoration;
- a place for prayer and devotion, both communal and personal;
- a sign of the presence of the Church within the local community ('a special sign of the pilgrim church on earth' (RDC 2));
- a place of cultural and social memory both for the Church and the wider community;
- a place of pilgrimage, to shrines or for particular devotions;
- a place of interest to society more generally because of its historical, artistic or architectural significance;
- a sign of the power and majesty of the Kingdom of God ('a sign and symbol of heavenly realities' (RDC 3)).

114. The Introduction to the Rite of Dedication of a Church says of the church building, 'the general plan...should be such that in some way it conveys the image of the gathered assembly...' (RDC 3, cf. GIRM 294, CTM 93). As the Liturgy is the action of the whole Church, so all its members should be able to participate fully according to their particular roles, whether gathering around altar, font or coffin, processing to Communion, or being reconciled with God and the Church. The shape and ordering of the building should be derived from what is required to celebrate the rites of the Church.

The primary function of the church building is to be a place where the local Church comes together to celebrate the Sunday Eucharist, when the two tables of the Word and Lord's Supper provide the main focus of action, around which the people gather (GIRM 28, cf. CTM 19–21). It is this form of worship for which the church building is primarily designed, however that design also needs to allow for the worthy celebration of the Paschal Triduum and in particular the Easter Vigil, and of other rites such as weddings and funerals.

115. Whenever possible the church building should be arranged so that there is sufficient space for all the elements of the rites to be carried out in a prayerful and reverent way, allowing their meaning to be clearly expressed.

116. Thus there should be good processional routes:

- for the priest and ministers, from the sacristy to the church door and the sanctuary;
- from the altar (where the Gospel book is placed at the beginning of Mass) to the ambo;
- for the people taking part in the procession with the gifts;
- for the communion procession;
- for baptismal parties to move from place to place as indicated in the rite, in particular from the font to the altar;
- for wedding and funeral parties from the door of the church to the places where they will be during the Liturgy;
- for praying the Stations of the Cross and other devotions.

117. Processional routes and all access routes in the Church must be made usable by as many people as possible. Reasonable provision must be made under the Disability Discrimination Act for all services and locations in a church to be accessible to those with disabilities. So, for instance, passages, aisles, gangways and entrances should be suitable for wheelchair and assisted walking access. Steps should be avoided where practicable and rails provided where appropriate.

118. *There should be suitable clear space close to the sanctuary:*

- for communion under both kinds to be distributed in a dignified and reverent way;
- for priests and ministers to prostrate themselves before the altar on Good Friday;
- for Rites of Christian Initiation, including parish confirmations;
- for weddings;
- for the coffin and the Paschal candle at funerals;
- for ordination rites.

2. The liturgical assembly

119. *Christ is always present in his Church, especially in its liturgical celebrations. He is present in the sacrifice of the Mass, not only in the person of his minister, 'the same now offering, through ministry of priests, who formerly offered himself on the cross,' but especially under the eucharistic elements. By his power he is present in the sacraments, so that when a man baptises it is really Christ himself who baptises. He is present in his word, since it is he himself who speaks when the holy Scriptures are read in the Church. He is present, lastly, when the Church prays and sings, for he promised: 'Where two or three are gathered together in my name, there I am in the midst of them' (Mt 18:20).*

SC 7

120. *To promote active participation, the people should be encouraged to take part by means of acclamations, responses, psalmody, antiphons and songs, as well as by actions, gestures and bearing.*

SC 30

121. *[So that the ministers and the faithful may more fully receive the good effects of the Mass], the entire celebration is planned in such a way that it leads to a conscious, active, and full participation of the faithful both in body and in mind, a participation burning with faith, hope, and charity, of the sort which is desired by the Church and demanded by the very nature of the celebration, and to which the Christian people have a right and duty by reason of their Baptism.*

GIRM 18

122. *The liturgical assembly is never a random group of individuals but the gathering of God's people to exercise its royal priesthood in the sacrifice of praise. Everything in the celebration is organised to encourage and foster an awareness of this assembly's common dignity and purpose, mutual interdependence, and connectedness with the wider Church.*

CTM 23

123. *The general plan of a church must be such that in some way it conveys the image of the gathered assembly. The people of God gathered together at Mass possess a coherent and hierarchical structure, expressed by different ministries and a different action for each part of the celebration. The general plan should also allow all the participants to take the place most appropriate to them and should encourage the proper carrying out of each one's role.*

CTM 93

124. Each baptised person is first and foremost a member of the assembly of the Church.

Each person exercising a particular ministry has his or her proper place within the arrangement of the assembly, not because of their status, importance or power as such, but because of the ministry they perform within and for the assembly.

- *The bishop or priest* leads the eucharistic celebration, presiding from his chair in the sanctuary (GIRM 310, CTM 99).
- *The deacon* sits close to the presider, traditionally on a stool or chair next to him (GIRM 174).
- *Concelebrants* When Mass is concelebrated seats are needed for all concelebrants but their arrangement should leave no confusion as to which minister is in fact presiding at the Liturgy (GIRM 207). Confusion may be avoided by placing concelebrants' seating in another place within the sanctuary, on another level or (if there is not sufficient space in the sanctuary) even in the body of the church. The placing of the concelebrants should enable them to carry out their ministry, but not impede other ministers nor obscure the assembly's view of the actions performed in the sanctuary (GIRM 215).

The Presidential Chair

125. *The chair of the priest celebrant must signify his office of presiding over the gathering and of directing the prayer. Thus the best place for the chair is in a position facing the people at the head of the sanctuary, unless the design of the building or other circumstances impede this: for example, if the great distance would interfere with communication between the priest and the gathered assembly, or if the tabernacle is in the centre behind the altar.*

GIRM 310

126. This chair symbolises the unity, leadership and service of the assembly gathered in Christ. The presiding bishop or priest leads the assembly in the Introductory Rite, the Collect and Post-Communion Prayers and the General Intercessions from the chair; it is also from there that he greets and dismisses the assembly, listens to the scriptures, and may also preach the homily. The location of the chair should enable the priest to be seen and heard by all in the assembly, and enable him in his exercising of his role as leader and servant of the community (CTM 99).

127. The chair is a key element in the general design of the sanctuary. It should be considered in relationship to the ambo and altar, and each of these should be given their own discrete space. The design of the chair may appropriately relate to the design of the ambo and altar, although it need not be made from the same material. The chair should not be a throne, but a seat for the one whose role is to preside at the Liturgy, whose leadership finds expression especially in a life of service.

The chair should be comfortable to sit in. If it is raised in some way, there should be enough space at and around it for the presider to stand, sit and kneel safely, as he is required to do by the various liturgical rites, and for the deacon's seat to be placed on the same level. Care should be taken also that there is sufficient space before the chair for rites such as Confirmation when candidates and sponsors will come to the bishop at the chair for the sacrament to be administered.

The chair may be blessed according to the rite provided in the *Book of Blessings* (BB).

128. If the presider will not be using a radio microphone, there should be provision at the chair for a microphone stand, ensuring that the microphone point is sited so as keep the amount of cable to a minimum.

129. It is not necessary that the chair should be fixed. It is, however, necessary that it should have a permanent place within the sanctuary. As with altar and ambo, the dignity of the chair demands that it not be obscured or cluttered with unnecessary items, although there should be somewhere suitable to keep hymnbook and notes, perhaps a small stool to the side. Space may also be necessary for a lectern (cf. 213 below).

A plain chair or stool for the Deacon should be provided where necessary.

Seating for lay ministers

130. *Servers* occupy benches, chairs or stools situated on the sanctuary or at least close to it, from where they can carry out their ministry with ease and dignity. Its positioning should make it clear that the servers are part of the gathered assembly. In most cases this will mean that servers sit forward of the presider and not behind him. They should not occupy deacons' places on either side of the presider (CTM 99).

131. *Musicians, choir director, cantor, animator* should be situated so that it is clear from their positioning they too are part of God's people gathered for worship, as well as providing them with a position which enables them to exercise their ministry of leading the assembly in its song. Often the choir director, animator or cantor may function as a link between the main body of the assembly and the choir and provision should be made for this if necessary.

Paragraphs 141–154 below give more detailed guidelines on provision for music and musicians.

132. *Readers, commissioned ministers of the Holy Communion and other lay ministers* are usually seated in the assembly; there is no need for them to be placed on the sanctuary.

Space and seating for the assembly

133. The church is a place of assembly and celebration. Seating needs to be provided for the assembly but of at least equal importance is the provision of space for the assembly (not only its principal ministers) to move around the church. There need to be aisles for processions, and places adequate for various liturgical actions which take place outside of the sanctuary – for example, certain rites of welcome and blessing, the presentation of gifts, the reception of Holy Communion.

Full and generous provision needs to be made for these actions. In Christian worship the assembly is performative not passive. In older churches, however, care needs to be taken as pews and other fixed seating may be of considerable quality or contribute positively to the character of the building.

134. *The people* assembled in the main body of the church should be provided with seating, which may be benches, pews or chairs. The decision as to which form(s) of seating should be used in a particular church may be influenced by many factors: the need for flexible use of the worship space; the age and relative mobility of the congregation; size of the congregation and the total space available; architectural/heritage issues; cost.

135. The layout of the seating should be a reminder that the Christian assembly is a gathered community, celebrating together as the Body of Christ. This is quite distinct from a gathering of individuals in a particular place for their private devotion, and who simply happen to be together at the same time. Seating arrangements which encourage people to sit apart from their brothers and sisters in Christ or which encourages people to watch passively should be avoided. As far as possible, the members of the assembly should be able to see the faces of those others gathered with them. As far as possible, all the assembly should be able clearly to see the sanctuary, the priest and ministers, and clearly to hear the presider, the readers, the cantor and choir (GIRM 311, CTM 21–24).

The space between the seats and rows should be sufficient to allow people to stand, kneel and sit in comfort. They should also be able to move freely during the Liturgy, for example, turning to face the entrance doors during the Rite of Entry of the RCIA or weddings and funerals, taking part in processions to communion, for ashes, to venerate the Cross on Good Friday, and to enter and leave the building in safety. It should be borne in mind that not everyone will leave their place to take part in the communion procession etc. and care should be taken for easy access to aisles without inconvenience to those who remain.

136. Space for wheelchairs and pushchairs should be allowed for in the overall seating plan and not simply left to fill convenient gaps.

137. The seating arrangements in the main body of the church should also take into consideration the requirements of celebrations and events other than Sunday Mass. For example, a good proportion of seats should also have a view of the baptistery.

138. It will often be convenient if some of the church's seating is in the form of chairs which can be removed or rearranged to better meet the needs of particular liturgies, for example gatherings at the font for baptism, or the sprinkling of a coffin; for a celebration of the Word or for the Liturgy of the Hours.

More flexible arrangements are possible if the nave of the church is not filled with fixed seating. It is also worth considering how much of the seating presently provided is habitually in use and removing some if this can be done. However, sensitivity should be exercised in the case of old seating where this is of good workmanship or part of the overall stylistic value of the church.

Since weekday services are generally less well attended, particular attention should be provided as to how to provide seating arrangements for these services which will encourage the community to draw together, rather than spreading to the extremities of the church.

139. *Kneelers*, where provided, should be spaced so as to enable people to stand and sit in comfort and to move in and out along rows of seats with ease. Movable kneelers will create noise as they are raised and lowered; fixed kneelers require more space for safe access to and from the seating. Hassocks may be an acceptable alternative in some situations.

140. *Floor surfaces* should be very carefully considered. Stone, wood, ceramic or resilient flooring may be more suitable than carpet, which may make a church feel warmer and add to the colour and texture, but may lead to problems: dust and dust mites trigger asthma in many people; absorbent surfaces such as carpet affect the way sound travels; some surfaces can impede wheelchair access, and condensation beneath may actually damage the floor surface, which is a particular problem if the church or floor is of artistic or historic merit.

Floor design may be part of the overall design of a church. In this case its retention and visibility should normally be ensured. In the case of listed buildings, and churches of artistic and architectural merit, advice (including that of the Historic Churches Committee where appropriate) should be sought and followed.

Any changes in floor level should be clearly marked.

Music and musicians

141. *The choir should be positioned with respect to the design of each church so as to make clearly evident its character as a part of the gathered community of the faithful fulfilling a specific role. The location should also assist the choir to exercise its role more easily and conveniently allow each choir member full, sacramental participation in the Mass.*

GIRM 312

142. The Liturgy includes many elements which are meant to be sung by the whole assembly or by priest, cantor or psalmist. This should be taken into consideration when dealing with the acoustics of the whole building.

143. The choir and musicians are part of the assembly and so they should be located within the body of the church, where they can support the people in their singing and also take a full part in the Liturgy as baptised Christians (CTM 43). There should be good visibility to the altar, ambo and president's chair and clear access to the communion procession. In order to lead the people, the choir, or at least the animator, should be visible to the rest of the people and the sound they produce should be clearly audible.

Space dedicated for the use of musicians should not act as a barrier to the assembly and the liturgical action, particularly when it is not being used.

144. The ministry of singers and musicians is to lead and encourage. Necessary activities such as tuning instruments or turning to the next piece of music should not be so visible as to be distracting.

145. *Psalmist* The responsorial psalm is part of the Liturgy of the Word, and so the psalmist should normally sing it from the ambo (or another suitable place, GIRM 61). The General Intercessions may also be sung from the ambo. The route to the ambo from the choir should be clear, and the psalmist should be able to approach the ambo easily and visibly from the assembly.

146. *Cantor/animator. Cantors* lead the singing at other points in the Liturgy; the penitential rite, litanies, the entrance and communion chant and other music. These are sung not from the ambo but from a separate place which is visible and audible to the assembly (using a microphone if necessary) while also close to the choir. The cantor may also minister as an *animator* to guide and encourage the people in their singing. A simple and portable music stand may be used but there should be no confusion between it and the ambo.

147. *Music director* The music or choir director must be visible to the whole choir and the organist or instrumentalists. If the music director also animates the assembly he or she should be visible to the people as well.

148. *Choir* There should be space for the whole choir to stand, sit, kneel and move about in order to take part fully in the Liturgy. All should have a clear view of the director and the liturgical action. (GIRM 312). Seating should be flexible and space included for music stands if necessary. Carpet should be avoided if possible.

149. *Instruments* Singers are frequently (but not always) supported by instruments. The task of such instruments is to sustain the choir and the people in the Church's song.

Traditionally the principal instrument used has been the organ but in recent years a variety of instruments have come to be used within the Liturgy (cf. *Music in the Parish Mass*, (MPM) 116).

150. The organ and other instruments are to be placed in an appropriate place so that they can sustain the singing of both the choir and the congregation and be heard with ease by all if they are played alone (GIRM 313).

More portable instruments will often be able to be played alongside the singers without making any particular demands on the space provided for the choir.

151. If the music is led by a music group or individual instrumentalists, space needs to be provided for music stands, electric points for instruments and task lighting and if necessary provision for amplification of instruments. It may be preferable for the musicians to use a different amplification circuit from that used by the presider, readers and psalmist, and the advice of an expert should be sought.

152. *In the Latin Church the pipe organ is to be held in high esteem, for it is the traditional musical instrument that adds a wonderful splendour to the Church's ceremonies and powerfully lifts up the spirit to God and to higher things.*

SC 120

The Organ Even when the pipework of an organ is elsewhere in the building it may be possible to have the console in a place where it is more connected with the choir or cantor. Alternatively, a reordering may be the appropriate time to consider the purchase of a new organ.

A national register of historic organs is maintained. In cases where restoration or enlargement or other works are being considered, the advice of an organ specialist (the organ advisor of the diocesan art and architecture committee or the Historic

Churches Committee) should be sought. It should also be remembered that the historic interest of an instrument resides both in its mechanical parts (pipes and moving parts) and in its ornamental casing.

153. In those cases where the organ console remains in an organ loft, it is rare that the choir also needs to be placed in the same loft. In most cases careful planning and coordination make it possible for the choir to be located within the same general area as the rest of the assembly

154. If a new organ is proposed, care should be taken that the console is not positioned where it will distract attention from the altar, ambo or presidential chair. It may be possible to install it slightly below floor level to achieve this. The casing should be in keeping with the style of the building; the sanctuary should not be dominated by organ pipes and care should be taken to ensure that any large speakers are placed sensitively in the church, and indeed be concealed where this is possible.

The need for supporting the Church's song at a wide range of different liturgical celebrations means that care should be taken to make possible good communication between the organist and other ministers. This may be assisted by placing the organ console with a clear view of the sanctuary and the entrance doors of the church or, if this is impossible, by providing a closed-circuit camera or a system of light signals.

An organ may be blessed according to the rite provided in the *Book of Blessings*.

Pastoral needs

155. In a worshipping community there will be a number of liturgical, catechetical and pastoral situations which require some sort of provision inside or close to the church building. These might include:

- space for parents and for infants and small children both within the main assembly and in a separate 'respite space';
- access and suitable space and other provision for members of the assembly who are disabled in particular ways;
- a place set aside for catechumens and catechists during the RCIA process (i.e. a *catechumeneon*);
- places for Liturgy of the Word with children;
- a crèche.

156. *Parents with infants and small children*

Parents and children are members of the assembly and should be encouraged to take their proper place. This means ensuring good access for prams and pushchairs into the church. Thought should be given as to how to provide for the safekeeping of prams and pushchairs during Liturgy.

Many parishes have created 'cry chapels' which parents and children are encouraged to use routinely. However, to deliberately set out to segregate a group of the baptised in this way is not good practice. Also many of these chapels are placed at the rear of the building, often with bad visibility and poor sound quality, and thus turn into noisy, chaotic places where many parents would rather not go at all.

There is an alternative to such an approach. Many other societies (including the societies of origin of many who are part of our parish communities) are far more tolerant of infants than is common in England and Wales. These societies do not view their children as distractions or annoyances, but as members of the community, welcome as a sign of promise for the future, and of blessing in the present. There may be something for those native to England and Wales to learn from this attitude. At the same time, all parents may be grateful to have a more private 'last resort' space where, for a brief time, they can give all their attention to comforting a baby or calming a toddler's tantrum.

If it is thought helpful to provide a place where restless children may be taken temporarily, then care should be taken to ensure that those who need to be there clearly remain part of the whole assembly able to participate in as much of the worship as is possible.

In any space intended for this purpose the following should be achieved, as far as is possible:

- easy access so that parents can slip in and out of the cry chapel without fuss and are far more likely to return to the body of the church at an early opportunity;
- good visibility to and from the main body of the church and the sanctuary;
- the sound system should be extended into the area (including amplification of organ, and musicians, also the church's loop system);
- 'child friendly' access, seating and floor coverings - for example, that there are no sharp edges at the head-height of a small child;
- a liturgical/prayerful ambiance that says that what takes place here is part of the Church's Liturgy.

157. *People with disabilities, their families and helpers.*

As full and equal members of the assembly, people with disabilities are entitled to participate fully in the Liturgy, including as liturgical ministers. The following are some of the matters that should be taken into consideration in order to assist such participation:

- In line with current legislation, access routes into and within the building should be wide enough for wheelchairs and be kept clear. Where at all possible, wheelchair users should be enabled to enter the building through the main door rather than a side entrance.
- Careful consideration should be given to the provision of easy alternative access routes (e.g. ramps and lifts) where there are stepped areas inside and outside the church. The provision of access to enable disabled people to play their full part as members of the assembly and in serving as liturgical ministers, for example in proclaiming the Word, it is to be commended.

- As far as possible floors should be even and changes of level clearly indicated for those with sight problems.
- Where it is necessary to retain steps inside or outside of the building consideration should be given to providing handrails.
- Careful lighting, bright but without glare, especially of access routes, helps those with failing sight.
- Seating should be made available for people who may need to sit close to the entrance. Those in wheelchairs should be able to sit alongside their families, friends or carers.
- Toilet facilities, when provided, must be accessible to everyone.
- All parts of the church, including the sanctuary, should be served by a loop system to enable people wearing hearing aids to listen to the spoken and sung parts of the Liturgy. Priests and readers should be clearly visible and adequately lighted to enable lip readers to understand what is being proclaimed.

The report *Valuing Difference: People with disabilities in the life and mission of the Church* (VD) (Bishops' Conference of England and Wales, 1998) includes sections on Liturgy and the sacraments. It also includes an *Audit of local church life* which give guidance on making proper provision for disabled people. New church buildings should take full account of these requirements. In many older churches it may not be possible to make every alteration which is suggested, but in all cases care should be taken to ensure equal access for all is provided so far as the constraints of the building, and parish budgets allow. The Disability Discrimination Act (1995), especially Part M *Building Regulations*, requires that by October 2004, all churches must have made 'reasonable adjustments' to enable physical access to all.

158. *Catechumeneon*

The Rite of Christian Initiation of Adults (RCIA) indicates that during the Catechumenate those who are preparing to be baptised during the Easter season should be dismissed from the assembly with their catechists in order to reflect on the scripture readings they have just heard. Thus there should be a suitable room close by the main body of the church in which this group may meet, a room conducive to prayer and reflection. This room is sometimes referred to as a *Catechumeneon*.

159. *Liturgy of the Word with children*

Where the Liturgy of the Word is celebrated with children apart from the assembly, there should be a suitable room close to the main body of the church to which the children and their leaders may process in safety.

3. Coming into the Church: Entrance and Narthex

160. *He is the Good Shepherd;*
he is the door through which those who follow him
enter and are safe, go in and go out, and find pasture.

Prayer of Blessing for new church doors, BB, 1229

161. *In the liturgical celebrations of baptism, marriage, and funerals provision is made for a rite of reception at the doors of the Church. On certain days of the liturgical year, the faithful pass through these doors in procession in to the body of the church. It is proper, then, in construction, design, and decoration church doors should stand as a symbol of Christ, who said: 'I am the door, whoever enters through me will be safe', and of those who have followed the path of holiness that leads to the dwelling place of God.*

Introduction to the Blessing of new church doors, BB, 1216

Principles

162. The doors of a church indicate the place of access. They should also be constructed in such a fashion as to make secure the church when it is left unattended.

163. The doors of the church, particularly the main doors, and the narthex, the space at the entrance to the church building, together form a threshold which people cross as they make the transition from the ordinary world to the worshipping community. They mark out a place where the stranger will begin their encounter of the Church at prayer and the place where the Church will formally welcome the stranger who seeks admission not just to the building but to the community of the Church. Thus it is at the entrance to the church that those seeking membership of the Christian community are admitted into the Order of Catechumens (RCIA 48); that baptismal and wedding parties are welcomed as they approach the sacraments; here too families grieving the loss of a loved one are greeted and the coffins of the deceased are sprinkled with holy water as a reminder of their first dying in Christ in baptism which contains the promise that in this second death they will rise with him in glory. Every Sunday this place of entry to the church is a place of welcome and greeting for the community. Here the community provides itself and its visitors with aids to participation in its Liturgy:

hymnbooks and service sheets. Here the community provides information of other dimensions of its common life; parish newsletters are distributed and notices displayed.
The doors may be blessed according to the rite provided in the *Book of Blessings*.

Practicalities

164. The main doors of the church should be substantial. This quality may be made manifest by their size and the materials of their construction. Provision should be made that the size and weight of the doors do not make access difficult to any of those who may wish to enter the church. Particular consideration should be given to access of those in wheelchairs or with another disability. Electronic systems for opening doors can be of great assistance. It is usually more suitable that these be operated manually than by an automatic system.

165. An open door is a potent sign of welcome. Where it is a practice made use of by the parish, thought should be given to how the open doors are secured and how, in the winter, heat is conserved. The use of glass doors can also be inviting but care should be taken with regard to safety.

166. Traditionally the surround of the door and the door itself have proved suitable for rich adornment alerting those entering of the significance of the church and the faith celebrated within it.

167. The height and width of the principal entrances needs to allow for their being used during the various entrance processions of the Church's year, for the dignified processing of the processional cross, banners, etc.

The narthex should therefore be large enough to allow not just the priest and ministers but a group of the faithful to gather for the rites of entry set out in different celebrations; the Church 'goes out to meet' those coming through its doors. (See Appendix A: 1, 5, 12, 13; 26, 33)

168. The processional route through the narthex should be clear and unobstructed; the way in and out of the church building should in any case give safe access for large numbers of people entering and leaving.

169. The space should be well lit, preferably with natural light.

170. Unless the font stands at or near the entrance there should be one or more holy water stoups close to the entrance for people to bless themselves as a reminder of their baptism. The water in these should be kept clean and replenished regularly. Where there is no font, for example in a retreat house or a religious or school chapel, the stoups should be of a size and design to call the sacrament of baptism to mind. During the Triduum holy water stoups are emptied, cleaned and dried.

171. In some areas, while it is not possible to keep the church open throughout the day, it may be possible to allow access to the narthex for people's private prayer at the church, even while the main part of the church is kept locked. Such provision is most usually made only when the tabernacle can be seen from the narthex.

172. When the narthex is also used as an 'information point', with noticeboards and newspapers for sale, care should be taken to ensure that clutter is kept in check, that information is kept up-to-date and in good condition, and that there are safe receptacles for money and alms which are emptied regularly. Often a parish's life is reflected in the state of its notices! Where a church is visited or worshipped in by different language groups it is appropriate that some of the information about the church and the parish should be in relevant languages.

173. *Refreshments* In some parishes, where there is a large narthex or porch, refreshments are served after the parish Mass in the narthex. When such a large narthex is lacking, and where there is no other suitable provision, such refreshments may even be provided at the back of the church itself. Where this happens care should be taken to respect the spiritual and liturgical aspects of the space, by clearing away equipment when it is not in use and keeping the space clean and tidy.

174. *The repository* The narthex is often, but not necessarily, the place where religious goods are sold. Care should be taken that fittings are suitable for the setting and do not detract from or interfere with the liturgical gathering space.

4. Proclaiming the Word: The Ambo

175. *May the Word of God always be heard in this place,*
as it unfolds the mystery of Christ before you
and achieves your salvation within the Church.

Liturgy of the Word, RDC 53

176. *When the Sacred Scriptures are read in the Church, God himself speaks to his people, and Christ, present in his own word, proclaims the Gospel.*

GIRM 29

177. *Christ is present in his word; as he carries out the mystery of salvation, he sanctifies us and offers the Father perfect worship... That word constantly proclaimed in the Liturgy is always, then, a living, active work through the power of the Holy Spirit. It expresses the Father's love that never fails in its effectiveness towards us.*

Introduction, *Lectionary for Mass* (LM) 4

178. *The dignity of the word of God requires that the church have a place that is suitable for the proclamation of the word and towards which the attention of the whole congregation of the faithful naturally turns during the Liturgy of the Word.*

GIRM 309

179. *The dignity of the ambo requires that only a minister of the word should make use of it. The ambo is used exclusively for the proclamation of God's word in the Scriptures, including the singing of the responsorial psalm; the elucidation and application of the word in the Homily and general intercessions; and also the Easter proclamation (*Exsultet*).*

CTM 98

Principles

180. The place for the proclamation of the word should normally be a fixed ambo and not simply a moveable lectern (GIRM 309). The place from which the Word is proclaimed needs to be 'somewhat elevated, fixed, and of a suitable design and nobility. It should reflect the dignity of God's word and be a clear reminder to the people that in the Mass the table of God's word and of Christ's body is placed before them. The place for the readings of the word must also truly help the people's listening and attention during the Liturgy of the Word. Great pains will therefore be taken, in keeping with the design of each church, over the harmonious and close relationship of the [ambo] with the altar.' (LM 32, CTM 98)

181. There should be only one ambo in the church, and all readings from the Scriptures, including the psalm whenever possible, should be proclaimed from it. Where a church has two fixed lecterns as once required in the Roman Rite only one of these should be used as an ambo, for the proclamation of the word. The other might be used for announcements or by the cantor, but its now lesser function might be able to be indicated in some way – for example by ensuring that any decoration of the ambo is not automatically mirrored by decoration of the former ambo, now the lectern for the cantor. Consideration might also be given to the removal of the former second lectern during a process of reordering.

An ambo should be blessed according to the rite provided in the *Book of Blessings*.

182. Consideration should be given to the ambo being large enough for several readers to use it together at the reading of the Passion on Palm Sunday and on Good Friday (LM 34).

183. *Relationship between ambo, altar and presidential chair*

The ambo should be what it is: a place for proclamation of the Word, and not a miniature altar.

The relationship between the altar and ambo may be shown by both being made from the same materials, and sharing some aspects of design, but they should not be made to look the same as one another, for they have different functions. It should be clear what liturgical action takes place at each location.

The presidential chair should be situated in a place which enables the presider to attend to the readings while they are proclaimed (see n. 125).

Practicalities

184. The *reading surface* should be angled and large enough to comfortably hold the book of the Gospels. At the bottom edge there should be a lip deep enough to hold the book in place.

185. Provision should be made for a *microphone* which may be discreetly incorporated in the design of the ambo which allows for pages of the Lectionary or Book of the Gospels to be turned (see section 17 Sound Amplification).

186. Suitable *lighting* should be directed on the ambo so that the reader may clearly see the page and so that the reader may be clearly seen by the assembly. The visibility of the reader is particularly important for those who rely on lip reading. On occasions where there is little or no electric light, for example the Easter Vigil, or Advent liturgies, suitable discreet lighting should also be provided.

187. Provision should be made to allow the easy use of the ambo by readers of different height; examples of how this may be achieved include:

- a means of altering the height or angle of the reading surface;
- space for a temporary step;
- a fold-down step incorporated in the design for the use of children and others.

Where possible, provision should be made for a reader in a wheelchair, considering issues of access, space and reading height.

188. *Sufficient space* should be allowed for dignified access and movement to and around the ambo on occasions when there is a number of people or items gathered there, for example:

- acolytes at the Gospel, or candles placed to each side;
- a minister with thurible;
- the Paschal Candle throughout the Easter season.

189. A *shelf* may be incorporated in the design to hold the Lectionary (when the Gospel book is used) and homily notes. This should not be visible to the assembly.

The *Evangelarium* is a place which enables a permanent display of the Book of the Gospels. It is a means of giving continued ritual significance to the Gospel book after the proclamation of the Gospel at Mass, and outside of liturgical services.

190. *Respect for setting*

A new ambo should respect the style, scale and materials of the building in which it will be set. It should complement liturgically and aesthetically the setting into which it is placed but it does not need to match its architectural style exactly. Reusing existing but otherwise redundant elements is one way of achieving this, but one which needs to be considered carefully.

191. *Retention/reuse of existing pulpit*

If the existing pulpit in the church is part of the overall church interior design, or is of architectural, artistic or historic merit, it should be retained. If it is possible to reuse it without significant alteration to serve the Liturgy (i.e. as an ambo), this should be the preferred option.

If it is considered that the pulpit will not adapt satisfactorily for liturgical use, competent advice should be sought. In the case of a listed building this must include the Historic Churches Committee, as any removal will require a faculty. The removal of such an item should only be considered as a last option.

5. A Holy and Living Sacrifice: The Altar

192. *Bless this altar built in the house of the Church,
that it may ever be reserved for the sacrifice of Christ,
and stand for ever as the Lord's table,
where your people will find nourishment and strength.
Make this altar a sign of Christ
from whose pierced side flowed blood and water,
which ushered in the sacraments of the Church.
Make it a table of joy,
where the friends of Christ may hasten
to cast upon you their burdens and cares
and take up their journey restored.
Make it a place of communion and peace,
so that those who share the body and blood of your Son
may be filled with his Spirit
and grow in your life of love.
Make it a source of unity and friendship,
where your people may gather as one
to share your spirit of mutual love.
Make it the centre of our praise and thanksgiving
until we arrive at the eternal tabernacle,
where, together with Christ,
high priest and living altar,
we will offer you an everlasting sacrifice of praise.*

Prayer of Dedication of an Altar, *Rite of Dedication of a Church and an Altar,* (RDA) 48

193. *At the altar the memorial of the Lord is celebrated and his body and blood given to the people. Therefore the Church's writers have seen in the altar a sign of Christ himself. This is the basis for the saying: 'The altar is Christ'.*

RDA 4

194. *The altar on which the Sacrifice of the Cross is made present under sacramental signs is also the table of the Lord to which the People of God is called together to participate in the Mass, as well as the centre of the thanksgiving that is accomplished through the Eucharist.*

GIRM 296

Principles

195. *Position* The altar is the place provided for the Liturgy of the Eucharist to be celebrated in a dignified and graceful way. There should be in every church building a fixed altar, that is an altar attached to the floor and which cannot be moved. The altar should be situated in the sanctuary in a position which is a natural and central focus within the church, and should be freestanding, so that the Eucharist may be celebrated by the priest facing the people and with sufficient space on all sides that the priest and other ministers may walk around it easily (see GIRM 298, 299, *Inter Oecumenici* 91, RDA 8, CTM 97).

196. *Materials and design* The tradition of the Church is for the table (*mensa*) of a fixed altar to be made from natural stone. In the dioceses of England and Wales, it may alternatively be made of wood which is worthy, solid and well-crafted provided that the altar is structurally immobile. The supports or base for upholding the table may be made of any sort of material, provided it is worthy and solid (see GIRM 301).

197. The altar should be large enough to hold the items necessary for the celebration of the Liturgy of the Eucharist: most notably the bread and wine to be offered and the vessels containing them, together with the Roman Missal (CTM 97). It should also be large enough for the action of the Breaking of Bread to be performed with dignity.

It is important to ensure that the table has the depth necessary for all the necessary items to be laid out in front of the priest, rather than to his side. The design or shape of the altar, the bread and wine should be clearly visible to all (GIRM 307) and not obscured by bookstands or candles.

Whereas rectangular altars may be most familiar in the tradition of the Western Church the requirements of the current rites of the Church may be better served by square altars, which give the necessary greater depth to the table, without taking up as much space on the sanctuary as would a rectangular altar of the same depth.

The design of the altar must ensure that it enjoys its proper prominence in the sanctuary.

Only what is required for the celebration of the Mass may be placed on the *mensa* of the altar: namely, from the beginning of the celebration until the proclamation of the Gospel, the *Book of the Gospels*; then from the Presentation of the Gifts until the purification of the vessels, the chalice with the paten, a ciborium, if necessary, and, finally, the corporal, the purificator, the pall, and the Missal. In addition, microphones that may be needed to amplify the priest's voice should be arranged discreetly (See GIRM 306).

198. *Relics*

'It is fitting to continue the tradition in the Roman Liturgy of placing relics of martyrs and other saints beneath the altar.'

RDA 11

Following the tradition of the church, fixed altars may incorporate relics of saints (who need not be martyrs) (GIRM 302). The relics, properly authenticated by the Church, should be recognisable as parts of a human body and not be tiny scraps of bone (RDA 11). They are normally to be placed in an opaque container and placed beneath the table of the altar and not in the *mensa* itself.

199. *One altar in a church* The altar is a sign of the one Saviour and the one Eucharist of the Church (RDA 7); there should therefore be only one altar in a church.

However, when a church has an existing altar which cannot be used for Mass facing the people, or which is placed or constructed so that it makes the participation of the people difficult, or which is of artistic or historic significance and thus cannot be removed a second new fixed freestanding altar of artistic merit should be constructed. In such cases this new altar alone should be used for the celebration of the Liturgy, and it should be made entirely clear that it is this new altar alone that is being so used (GIRM 303).

It is also highly desirable that the new altar be properly dedicated, in accordance with the Rite for Dedication of an Altar. (Where permission has been given for a moveable altar this too may be dedicated, though it is permissible for it simply to be blessed) (GIRM 300). The inclusion of relics from the old altar in the new one will emphasise that there is no sense of compromise or expediency involved in the new arrangement, and it will ensure a feeling of continuity with the traditions of the community. Before relics are removed from a former altar, however, consideration should be given to its historic or artistic integrity. The advice of the Diocesan Art and Architecture Committee should be sought. If the altar is in a listed building, a faculty from the Historic Churches Committee will be necessary for such removal.

This primary role of the new altar may be established architecturally and also by not decorating the old altar in any special way. Even if the old altar is used as the place of reservation of the Eucharist, the veiled tabernacle and the lamp burning before it should indicate that this is a place of reservation, not of celebration. Even in the case of the old altar being the place of reservation it is inappropriate for lit candles, flowers and altar cloths to be used on or around it (GIRM 303, *Ceremonial of Bishops* (CB) 48).

200. *Side altars* In older churches any side altars fixed to the wall or to integral altarpieces may no longer be used as altars. However they should be retained if they are of particular artistic or historic merit or if they serve as shrines for devotion. Any proposals which do not follow this general principle would need sound justification. It may be suitable for the eucharistic reservation to be relocated to one of these where it is possible to create there a suitable and reverent place for private prayer. (see also Section 9 on the Reservation of the Blessed Sacrament)

Practicalities

201. *Space* The altar is a sign of Christ; it is a most holy symbol (RDC 4).

Where the altar stands on a raised area within the sanctuary, there should be enough space for all the ministers to gather around the altar (e.g. at Confirmation, the Bishop, concelebrants and deacons); and for the altar to be incensed without the presider having to negotiate steps during the incensing. There should also be space around the altar for the placing of candlestands and flowers.

202. *Cross* The Paschal Mystery celebrated in the eucharistic liturgy was accomplished through the Crucifixion and Resurrection. Christians glory in the cross of the Lord (see *Galatians* 6:14). As a constant reminder of the cost of salvation and the symbol of Christian hope, the cross should be visible to the entire assembly during the Eucharist. It may be carried in procession, or there may be a fixed cross on or near the altar (GIRM 308). Care should be taken not to multiply crosses in the place of worship and so detract from the effect of this symbol of the Paschal Mystery.

It is usual for this cross to bear a figure of Christ crucified. However, in the tradition of the Church the saving mystery of the Crucified One has been represented in different ways, sometimes by a figure of the suffering or dead Christ on the cross, sometimes by a figure showing the Resurrected Lord standing in triumph as King or High Priest at the cross; sometimes without representation of the person of the Lord but simply by a plain cross.

It is desirable that such a cross, recalling the saving Passion of the Lord, remain near the altar even outside of liturgical celebrations (CTM 103-104).

203. *Candles and decoration* Candles may be placed upon or near the altar, so long as they do not obscure the vessels and the presider (GIRM 117, 307, CTM 114-115).

Flowers and other items should not be placed on the altar but around it (GIRM 305, CTM 118-121).

While it is sometimes pastorally desirable for posters, children's paintings and so on to be displayed within the Liturgy, these things should never be affixed to the altar. They are more appropriately displayed on simple stands or frames. These should be positioned so as not to detract from the liturgical action.

204. *Sound amplification* The use of a radio microphone is to be encouraged.

If it is necessary to install a microphone point, even as a backup system, consideration should be given to placing it discreetly below the *mensa* or in the floor surface rather than in the structure of the altar (GIRM 306).

The altar should not be used as a housing for a sound system.

205. *Historic considerations* These should be balanced with the liturgical and pastoral ones. This can be particularly important where an existing altar is of great artistic or historic merit.

It is permissible for the existing high altar to remain *in situ*, if on account of its design and setting within the sanctuary and the church it cannot be moved to another suitable position in the church (GIRM 303).

Some recent reorderings have adapted the old altar, perhaps by moving the *mensa* and its base forward to create a freestanding structure according to the norms, others have created a copy of the old altar standing forward from it. Usually, however, simply moving the *mensa* and base of the old altar forward destroys its proportions and historic unity, leaving the old reredos bereft, without a base. The provisions of GIRM 303 should be observed and a new and appropriate altar built and dedicated.

In such a case the advice of Historic Churches Committee should be sought.

6. A FOCUS FOR LOVING SERVICE: THE SANCTUARY

206. *The sanctuary is the place where the altar stands, where the word of God is proclaimed, and where the priest, the deacon, and the other ministers exercise their offices. It should suitably be marked off from the body of the church either by its being somewhat elevated or by a particular structure and ornamentation. It should, however, be large enough to allow the Eucharist to be celebrated properly and easily seen.*

GIRM 295

Principles

207. When the Church assembles to celebrate the Eucharist then in addition to Christ's presence in the assembly, Christ is also present in the person of the priest presiding, in the word proclaimed, and in the sacrament of his Body and Blood offered and shared. Thus the places associated with those actions - the altar, the ambo, the presidential chair – are natural focal points for the assembly called to full participation in them. The place for these three major focal points is the sanctuary, the distinctive part of the church where particular liturgical ministries of leadership and service have their place and are clearly shown.

The altar, ambo and chair should always be designed specifically to meet the particular function of each. At the same time the unity of the Eucharistic action as a whole should be indicated by the incorporation into the design of each of some elements of common or complementary design. The altar, ambo and chair should also be provided with the space necessary for the reverent carrying out of the liturgical actions proper to each:

- the altar and chair should be sufficiently far apart to enable the priest to preside from the chair and then move to the altar for the Liturgy of the Eucharist, returning to the chair for the Post-Communion Prayer, blessing and dismissal;
- the chair and ambo should be placed so that the presider can pay attention to the Word as it is proclaimed.

The arrangement of the sanctuary should reveal the relationship that exists between these three elements in the celebration of the Mass. For example there should be a clear and dignified processional route along which during the Liturgy of the Word the deacon or priest may move from the presidential chair to the altar then to carry the Gospel book in procession from the altar to the ambo. When a bishop presides at the Liturgy of the Word the Gospel book may be taken from the ambo to the Bishop at the chair, for him to venerate it there.

Practicalities

208. The sanctuary should be spacious enough for the rites to be celebrated with grace and reverence, and allow easy access for ministers to carry out their tasks properly. Particular consideration should be given to the position of the altar in relation to the other elements on the sanctuary and the ritual movements around them, for example incensations of altar, ministers and people.

209. Although it is an integrated part of the whole sacred space, the sanctuary should be marked, normally by a raised floor, its lighting and/or decoration, but not by rails (see 218 below). While the floor of the whole sanctuary may be higher than the rest of the church, fewer steps and changes in level around altar, ambo and chair will facilitate the reverent, graceful and safe performance of the Liturgy. Any raised floor levels or steps should be as few as necessary for good visibility and should not compromise the sanctuary's allowing for ease of movement even when, for example, the Book of the Gospels or a processional cross is being carried. Access for disabled ministers should also be considered as far as possible within any architectural or historic constraints imposed by the building.

210. Often work on *sound and heating systems* can be incorporated in any project involving alterations in floor levels (see also sections 17 and 18). Extra microphones may be required for particular celebrations, for example the reading of the Passion narratives: these should be easy to operate and to move unobtrusively. Microphones should not be left switched on when not in use.

211. In order that the principal focuses of altar, ambo and presidential chair stand out most clearly the sanctuary should be kept free from unnecessary furnishings and objects. However in order to enable the rites to be celebrated with ease and dignity some ancillary furnishings are necessary. These include:

- Seating, as required, for concelebrants, deacons (see 124) and servers (see 130);
- Provision for cantor/animator (see 146);
- Credence table(s);
- Other furnishings as required for particular celebrations (see below);
- Fixed historic furnishings should be given similar consideration to historic altars (cf. GIRM 303).

212. *Credence table* There should be a credence table on the side of the sanctuary large enough to hold the Missal, empty vessels, and all other things necessary for celebrating the rites. This table or another may also be the place where the cup is prepared or vessels are cleaned after Communion (GIRM 118).

213. *Lectern* Usually it is a server who should hold the Missal for the priest at the Introductory Rite and for the Prayer after Communion and any other books required at other times, for example at the Prayer of the Faithful. However on those occasions when a server is not available it may be necessary to provide a portable lectern to hold these books so that the priest can properly lead these presidential prayers from the chair. If a small lectern is used it should not resemble the ambo in dignity or decoration nor obscure the presider when he is seated.

214. *Use of Sanctuary space* Provision for the following should also be considered:

- space for processional cross stand;
- places by ambo and altar for candles (see 188, 197, 203);
- space by the ambo or elsewhere in the sanctuary for the Paschal Candle during the Easter season;
- space for flowers and other seasonal decorations;
- space for thurible stand.

215. Often hymn boards are placed in the sanctuary – as one of the natural focuses of the liturgical assembly. If this is necessary, care should be taken that the design of the board is in keeping with the rest of the sanctuary. It should be borne in mind that the board is not a liturgical fitting rather an aid to participation therefore when there is no need for the display of hymn numbers it should be taken away, or be of such a design that it does not attract the eye when the numbers have been removed.

216. *The reception of Holy Communion*

Receiving Holy Communion is a key action in the celebration of Mass. As a result of papal encouragement throughout the 20th Century it became more common for people to receive Holy Communion at Mass than was the case when many churches in England and Wales were built. The further reforms of the Second Vatican Council ensured that during the last quarter of the 20th Century communion was increasingly ministered under both kinds. These two developments concerning this important part of the Mass make significant demands on the provision of liturgical space.

217. The space provided for the distribution and reception of Holy Communion needs to be adequate for the movement of communicants and for a minimum of three ministers, one distributing the Body of the Lord, the others the Precious Blood. Often six or more ministers are necessary, and there should be room for all to stand at or near the entry to the sanctuary.

A clear processional route helps to ensure that the communion procession can take place in a reverent and prayerful manner.

- At the points where communion is ministered, there needs to be space for communicants to receive communion in a recollected manner, and with proper reverence.
- The reception of the Body of the Lord is often accomplished more quickly than the drinking from the chalice, thus, despite the presence of extra ministers, sometimes a queue for the chalice will develop. Space needs to be provided to allow for this.
- Communicants need also to be able to return to their place after communion, prayerfully, undistracted by wondering how they will do so.

218. Although the provision of altar rails was formerly customary it was not mandated by the Church. This remains the case: there is no liturgical requirement for *altar rails* in churches.

However where the Church is of historical or architectural significance, and altar rails are already in place and are an aspect of that historical or architectural significance, preference should be given to retaining the altar rails in place. Where there are pressing reasons for removal, the advice of the Diocesan Art and Architecture Committee should be sought and in the case of a listed building, that of the Historic Churches Committee.

219. At times during the history of the Church the sanctuary has been physically set apart from the space for the laity by architectural features such as rails, steps or screens. More recently it has become an integral part of the whole place of assembly which conveys 'a unity that is clearly expressive of the unity of the entire holy people' (GIRM 294). When reordering is contemplated the sanctuary should not be considered as a separated 'more holy' enclave but in terms of its place within the whole sacred space and its relationship with other important areas: the baptistery and reconciliation chapel; the entrance ways of priests and ministers and of the people; the reservation of the Blessed Sacrament and other areas for private prayer; clear and dignified processional routes. The rites expect that many actions — for example, processions and devotions, baptisms, reconciliation and funerals — will take place in other places in the building. All the rites, though, are linked to the celebration of the Eucharist, so the relationship of the sanctuary to the other ritual spaces within the building is of crucial importance.

7. Womb and Tomb: The Place for Baptism

220. *Father, you give us grace through sacramental signs,*
which tell us of the wonders of your unseen power.
In baptism we use your gift of water,
which you have made a rich symbol of the grace
you give us in this sacrament.

Prayer over the Water, Celebration of Baptism, RCIA 287A

221. *In the sacraments of Christian initiation we are freed from the power of darkness and joined to Christ's death, burial and resurrection. We receive the Spirit of filial adoption and are part of the entire people of God in the celebration of the memorial of the Lord's death and resurrection.*

Christian Initiation, General Introduction (CIGI) 1

222. *The baptistery or the area where the baptismal font is located should be reserved for the sacrament of baptism and should be worthy to serve as the place where Christians are reborn in water and the Holy Spirit.*

CIGI 25

Principles

223. The sacrament of Baptism is such an important event for the community of the Church, so rich in symbol and meaning, that even in the smallest churches the place for baptism should be kept distinct from other areas in the church. A separate, well-cared for and beautifully adorned baptistery with a font which through its design declares that all are welcome to the fountain of life, shows clearly the importance the church attaches to baptism. Even when a parish has few baptisms each year, it is important that there should be a permanent font in the parish church, as a constant reminder of the importance and meaning of baptism: the way to a new creation through water and the Holy Spirit.

A font should be blessed according to the rite provided in the *Book of Blessings*.

224. The baptismal Liturgy places a great emphasis on the entrance into the community of faith, the Church. Thus, while a baptism should be an occasion of great joy for the family most particularly involved, it is also a celebration for the local church community as a whole (RCIA 4, 9). Consequently it is expected that representatives of the community will be present at the baptism, or the baptism will take place during the Sunday Mass. It is also anticipated that more than one baptism may take place at a single celebration.

225. The baptismal rites for both adults and children take place at various locations in the church:

- the welcome or presentation of the candidates at the door or narthex;
- procession to the Liturgy of the Word at the ambo;
- procession to the font for the Rite of Baptism and its illustrative rites;
- procession to the altar in order to take part in or look forward to the eucharistic Liturgy around the altar.

Thus suitable space should be set aside for the baptismal party and at least some members of the church community to gather at the beginning of the Liturgy. This may be at the church door, in the narthex or in a place near the entrance of the church.

Consideration should be given to appropriate seating arrangements during the rite, for example for the whole assembly during the Liturgy of the Word, and for the elderly or infirm at other times during the celebration.

226. In some parish churches, portable fonts or bowls are regularly used for baptism, sometimes for what seem to be the best of reasons. However, these arrangements are most inadequate to indicate the great importance of this sacrament and the dignity that it confers upon the baptised. Parishes without a proper baptistery or at least a fixed font set apart for the celebration of the sacrament should seek to make such provision as soon as possible.

Where in exceptional situations the font is not able to be used, perhaps at the Easter Vigil, if the font is out of sight of the vast majority of the congregation, then a worthy vessel should be provided for the baptismal water, rather than a portable font.

227. *The baptistery* need not be a separate, enclosed place, but should always be a space which is recognisably distinct within the body of the church. If not an enclosed space, the baptistery should be differentiated by the use of colour, artwork, design or decoration. A change in flooring may be sufficient to define the baptistery area. Changes of level raise safety and access issues. One appropriate and traditional place is by or close to the entrance of the church.

The space around the font should be large enough for a number of people to gather, including several baptismal parties, as envisaged by the rite itself. A font is rarely acceptable in the sanctuary area as it is the place reserved for the celebration of the Eucharist. The aim should be to provide a separate, dedicated space for the sacrament of Baptism, but ensuring that the font is visible at least from part of the main body of the church.

228. *The baptismal font* is the focal point for the sacrament, standing as a permanent reminder of the baptismal vocation of the Christian community. The font is the container for the 'pure and clean' water used in baptism and should be 'spotlessly clean and of pleasing design' (CIGI 18).

229. *In the celebration of baptism the washing with water should take on its full importance as the sign of that mystical sharing in Christ's death and resurrection through which those who believe in his name die to sin and rise to eternal life.*

RCIA 206

230. *As the rite for baptising, either immersion, which is more suitable as a symbol of participation in the death and resurrection of Christ, or pouring may lawfully be used.*

CIGI 22

231. In the baptismal Liturgy preference is given to baptism by immersion (that is either by full immersion, or standing or kneeling in water while water is poured over the head and whole body) rather than by infusion (that is, leaning over a font or bowl as water is poured over the head). New fonts should be designed and sited to enable both methods to take place for both adults and children from any side. (This avoids any inconvenience to ministers be they left or right-handed.) Consequently the bowl of the font needs to be quite large in size. Where the immersion of adults is to be undertaken a sunken or raised pool will need to be incorporated, or at least a floor area with adequate drainage or able to contain the poured water.

Practicalities

232. The water in the font should be readily accessible for those other rites which require the use of baptismal water, for example the funeral rite, the Rite of Sprinkling at Sunday Mass or Baptismal Vespers on the evening of Easter Sunday.

233. For baptismal pools consideration will need to be given to how people will enter and leave the water safely, and to whether the presider will stand inside or outside the pool. In addition, how disabled people will baptise or be baptised, with any assistance necessary, should be considered. Consideration should also be given to where people will change into baptismal garments immediately afterwards. This might be the sacristy or a separate chapel or other room.

234. In the absence of a permanent pool the building or hiring of a temporary pool for baptisms at the Easter Vigil and during the Easter season is encouraged, as a step on the way to a more permanent arrangement for the celebration of baptism.

235. When a parish is considering the installation of a permanent immersion font, thought should be given to incorporating the existing font into it, provided that that font is of sufficient size and character to meet the requirements of the rite.

Where the existing baptistery is of architectural or historic significance and cannot be adapted to the demands of immersion baptism, the appropriateness of introducing into the church a second space dedicated to baptism should be carefully considered. (See 239 below). Where the church is listed, a faculty for any work must be sought through the Historic Churches Committee.

236. When a font or pool is installed careful consideration should be given to how it will be filled, emptied, cleaned and maintained, and the implications of drainage and heating. Running water may be supplied to the font (CIGI 21) so that this ancient and pure symbol may be used. However, a font with running water will involve careful consideration, such as whether the water will run constantly or only when required.

237. While the symbol of living water has a profound meaning for the Christian church, it is important to guard against any health and safety risk that a baptismal pool might introduce. People can drown in even a few inches of water. Parents with small children, especially, should be made aware of the potential hazard and encouraged to keep their children under supervision.

The provision of a suitable cover for the font or pool, besides keeping the water clean, may address some of these issues.

238. Some seating might be provided within the baptistery for those who may need it during the rite of baptism itself.

239. If the reordering of a church is likely to result in the disuse of an existing place of Baptism, the future use of that space will have to be carefully considered. While it may be possible to reuse a font no longer used for baptism as, for example, a holy water vessel at the Church entrance, the integrity of such a font must be safeguarded and respected. When the furnishings and embellishments of a former baptistery are so integral to it that they are to be retained care should be taken over its relationship to the new baptistery. The Diocesan Art and Architecture Committee and, where necessary, the Historic Churches Committee, should be consulted.

Storage of the Holy Oils

240. The holy oils blessed and consecrated by the bishop at the Chrism Mass are the oil of catechumens, the oil of the sick, and the oil of chrism. The oil of catechumens is used to anoint adults during the period of the catechumenate and to anoint adults and infants immediately before they are baptised. The oil of the sick is used to anoint those who suffer serious illness. The oil of chrism, an aromatic oil, is used to anoint those being initiated into the Church at their baptism and confirmation, to anoint bishops and priests at their ordination, and in the dedication of a church and altar. The use of these oils is one of the indications that all the liturgies in the local church are carried out by virtue of the bishop's authority and in communion with him. The greater attention to the authenticity of liturgical signs required by the Second Vatican Council means that oils are used more generously than was previously the case, consequently churches now store the holy oils in greater quantity.

241. It is appropriate for the holy oils used in the celebration of the sacraments of the Church to be housed close to the place where the sacraments of initiation are celebrated although this is not mandatory, thus strengthening the connection between baptism and other sacraments, especially confirmation.

242. The oils are kept in a cabinet, or aumbry, which is secure and of pleasing design and used only for storing the oils. The doors to the aumbry and indeed the containers themselves may be made of glass, so that the oils within are visible. It is inappropriate for a lamp to burn in front of the oils; they are reserved for use within sacramental worship rather than as a focus for worship in their own right.

An aumbry may be blessed according to the rite provided in the *Book of Blessings*.

243. Oil should be stored in sufficient quantity to ensure its generous use in the sacraments. The vessels used should be of a size and quality befitting their purpose.

244. Outside the season of Easter the Easter candle is kept in the baptistery, in such a way that candles for the newly baptised may be easily lit from it, and so that it may be conveniently moved when required elsewhere, for example to stand beside the coffin at a funeral. (See 310)

8. Celebrating the mercy of God: the place of Reconciliation

245. *Where sin has divided and scattered,*
may your love make one again;
where sin had brought weakness,
may your power heal and strengthen;
where sin has brought death,
may your Spirit raise to new life.

Chapter 4, Opening Prayer no.5 (99), *Rite of Penance* (RP)

246. *In the sacrament of Penance the faithful 'obtain from the mercy of God pardon from their sins against him; at the same time they are reconciled with the Church which they wounded by their sins and which works for their conversion by charity, example and prayer'.*

Introduction, no.4, RP

247. *Communal celebration shows more clearly the ecclesial nature of penance.*

Introduction, no.22, RP

Principles

248. In every church there should be a particular place designated for the celebration of the sacrament of Penance. This may be a separate reconciliation chapel or room or a more traditional confessional but this should be in an area which is open and visible (*Misericordia Dei* 28). As well as individual confession and reconciliation according to Rite 1, the Church commends communal services of penance and reconciliation following Rite 2, especially during Advent and Lent. Such communal celebrations take place in the main body of the church with suitable spaces identified for individual confessions which should also be in visible areas but without the possibility of confessions being overheard. At least one of these spaces should give penitents an alternative to celebrating the sacrament other than face-to-face with the priest (see below). In addition, the requirements of the Nolan Report on child protection should be put into practice.

A confessional or reconciliation chapel may be blessed according to the rite provided in the *Book of Blessings*.

249. The Rite of Penance may be celebrated either face-to-face or with the penitent separated from the confessor by a curtain or grille. A proper reconciliation room or other space should be established for the celebration of the sacrament of penance which is suitable for both these options. The Nolan Report recommends that the setting for reconciliation of children should be in a place where both priest and child may be seen but not heard (Nolan: 3.3.9 and Recommendation 25), and this arrangement is probably suitable for other penitents also. Access should be open to all, including those in wheelchairs and with hearing difficulties. The ancient option of celebrating this sacrament at the presider's chair might also be considered. Other possible solutions include:

- glass panels in the doors, or a window through which the priest and penitent may be seen (this is also useful for a parent who has to leave children outside). For alterations to traditional confessionals, see below, 255;
- the provision of more than one door, so that neither priest nor penitent may be trapped inside;
- the provision of a 'panic button' so that help may be summoned if necessary.

250. *Safety and security are both important considerations.* Those who celebrate the sacrament should be protected from allegations and even physical attacks; both priests and people can feel, and sometimes are, acutely vulnerable in this one-to-one situation. The arrangements should enable the rite to be celebrated in safety and integrity by both priest and penitent.

251. The reconciliation chapel is an important place for the Christian's encounter with Christ. As a liturgical space, it should express what it means to encounter the mercy and love of God, to be reconciled with the community of the Church even when not in use. It should be clearly visible within the church, although its location may be to some extent dictated by the architecture of an existing building.

252. Penitents are reconciled with the Church as well as with God; a way of encouraging people to make links between reconciliation and their life in the Church may be to locate the reconciliation room close to the font (or vice versa) thus associating reconciliation with the baptismal water through which sins are also forgiven. Another option might be to make some spatial link between the reconciliation room and the altar table; a return to the Church's primary celebration, the Eucharist.

Practicalities

253. When a penitent enters the reconciliation chapel he or she should not be faced with the priest at once; the choice of celebration belongs to the penitent. For face-to-face, there should be chairs for priest and penitent, a suitable distance apart, so that the priest can extend his hands over the head of the penitent (RP 19), but not so close that either feels in any way uneasy. It should be possible for the penitent to sit or kneel and to rise afterwards. A grille or curtain arrangement should also be provided with a kneeler or chair.

254. Other things to consider include:

- provision for the Scriptures to be read during the rite;
- soundproofing: a reconciliation chapel should be soundproofed for confidentiality; carpet will also contribute to the absorption of sound;
- the visibility of priest and penitent: priest and penitent should preferably be positioned at right angles to the viewing window or door to prevent inadvertent lip-reading or embarrassing eye-contact with those outside;
- easy access and provision for people with disabilities;
- the provision of natural light, if possible;
- the conversion of a side chapel into a reconciliation room with existing or new stained glass might be considered;
- the use of good quality furnishings in natural materials, which give dignity and importance to the rite;
- suitable art: a crucifix or an icon, not set up as a shrine or altarpiece but as a focus for prayer or reflection;
- adequate ventilation and heating;
- an indicator of whether or not a penitent is with the priest and a name board to identify the priest;
- the reconciliation chapel should not be used for other things, such as storage.

255. Where traditional confessionals are fine examples of design and craftsmanship, their adaptation if needed will require particular care. In all such cases, the advice of the Diocesan Art and Architecture Committee should be sought, and in the case of listed churches a faculty must also be obtained from the Diocesan Historic Churches Committee.

9. An abiding presence: reservation of the Blessed Sacrament

256. *The celebration of the eucharist in the sacrifice of the Mass is the true origin and purpose of the worship shown to the eucharist outside Mass. The principal reason for reserving the sacrament after Mass is to unite, through sacramental communion, the faithful unable to participate in the Mass, especially the sick and aged, with Christ and the offering of his sacrifice.*

In turn, eucharistic reservation, which became customary in order to permit the reception of communion, led to the practice of adoring this sacrament and offering to it the worship...which is due to God. This cult of adoration is based upon valid and solid principles.

Eucharistiae Sacramentum, (ES), 21 June 1973

257. *In order to give right direction and encouragement to devotion to the sacrament of the eucharist correctly, the eucharistic mystery must be considered in all its fullness, both in the celebration of Mass and in the worship of the sacrament reserved after Mass in order to extend the grace of the sacrament.*

Holy Communion and Worship of the Eucharist outside Mass (HCWE), 4

258. *In accordance with the structure of each church and legitimate local customs, the Most Blessed Sacrament should be reserved in a tabernacle in a part of the church that is truly noble, prominent, readily visible, beautifully decorated, and suitable for prayer.*

GIRM 314

The tabernacle

259. The Blessed Sacrament is reserved in the first place, so that communion and viaticum may be taken to the sick and the dying. Its reservation also affords a precious opportunity for the rest of the faithful for worship and adoration of the Lord's abiding presence (HCWE 5, CTM 101, RS 129).

260. The Blessed Sacrament should not be reserved on an altar which is used for the celebration of Mass (GIRM 315). In a new church a specially designed column, shelf, aumbry or tower should be constructed to hold a tabernacle. This option is also recommended for the reordering of an older church, though the tabernacle may also be set on an altar which is no longer so used, in its own space, apart from the altar of celebration (GIRM 303).

261. The tabernacle should be made of solid, unbreakable and opaque materials and should be securely bolted in place from the inside so it cannot be moved. It should be lockable and the key kept safe. In some circumstances it may be necessary to consider an alarm system for protection (GIRM 314, HCWE 10).

A tabernacle should be blessed according to the rite provided in the *Book of Blessings*.

262. Access to the tabernacle should be clear and safe for those who may need to take the Blessed Sacrament to the sick at any time, and for the reservation of any remaining hosts after Mass.

263. The size of the tabernacle should be considered carefully, both in relation to its surroundings and in the quantity of reserved hosts it can hold. The hosts reserved in the tabernacle are primarily for the communion of the sick, so in normal circumstances very few hosts need to be reserved. The tradition and practice of the church is that all should receive communion from the bread and wine consecrated at the mass at which they are present and not from the reserved Sacrament in the tabernacle (GIRM 85, 321).

264. In England and Wales a lamp burning before the tabernacle is the usual sign of the presence of the reserved Sacrament. So long as the Sacrament is reserved this lamp is kept lit as a sign of respect of the Lord's sacramental presence. By tradition the light is an oil lamp or a light with a wax candle (GIRM 316, HCWE 11, and see also CB 912, RDC 81).

265. Unless the design of the tabernacle is of particular artistic merit the tabernacle may be veiled.

266. The surface on which the tabernacle sits should extend forward sufficiently to accommodate a ciborium or a monstrance when removing or reposing the Blessed Sacrament. The tabernacle is not the place for exposition; the place for exposition is on the altar of sacrifice.

267. There should be only one tabernacle in a church (GIRM 314). However, many older churches have several old altars, each fitted with a tabernacle. If possible, these other tabernacles should be removed. Where an unused tabernacle is an integral part of an altar of artistic or historic interest it should be retained. One tabernacle should be designated as the regular and permanent place of reservation in the church, and any others, including, if applicable, the tabernacle on a former high altar, should not be dressed as though they were in use (for example, no flowers, cloths, veils or lights should draw attention to them). In such a case one of the other, generally unused, tabernacles may be used as the altar of repose during the Triduum. The advice of the Diocesan Art and Architecture Committee, and of the Historic Churches Committee in the case of a listed church, should be sought prior to any changes being implemented.

The place of reservation

268. The documents of the Church give two options for where the tabernacle may be placed.

- either in the sanctuary, apart from the altar of celebration, in a form and place more appropriate, not excluding on an old altar no longer used for celebration (GIRM 315);

or

- likewise, in some chapel suitable for private adoration and prayer of the faithful, which should be organically connected to the church and readily visible to the Christian faithful. (GIRM 315; RDC 79-82; HCWE 9; *Eucharisticum Mysterium* (EM) 53; CB 910-913, RS 130).

It should be noted that the Liturgy of the Paschal Triduum presumes that the place of reservation will normally be in a separate place from the sanctuary

269. Whenever the place of the reservation is being considered the advice of the Diocesan Art and Architecture committee or Liturgy Commission should be sought. In the case of buildings of historic or artistic significance competent advice should be sought from both artistic and liturgical sources and, where necessary, from the Historic Churches Committee.

The bishop of the diocese has ultimate responsibility for determining which of the two options is most appropriate in any particular circumstance.

Reservation in the sanctuary

270. The bishop of the diocese may give permission for the sacrament to be reserved in the sanctuary or even on a former altar, i.e. an altar no longer used for the celebration of Mass (GIRM 314).

271. The relationship of the reserved sacrament and the Liturgy of the Eucharist should be made clear by the liturgical arrangement of the Church. It should be clear to all that the reserved sacrament derives from the sacrifice offered and shared in during the Liturgy of the Eucharist. Such a clarity of understanding may be achieved through catechesis as well as by the appropriate use of artwork and decoration, as well as other aspects of church design. The main altar – the altar of celebration – should be the primary focus of the church, even when no Liturgy is taking place.

272. Where the Sacrament is reserved in a tabernacle which is part of an old high altar, that altar should not be used for the celebration of Mass, nor dressed with candles and altar cloths as though it were still in use, or decorated in any special way (GIRM 303). In such instances the provision of the tabernacle lamp itself is sufficient.

Reservation in a Blessed Sacrament Chapel

273. A separate Blessed Sacrament chapel should be in a conspicuous and distinguished place, secure and decorated appropriately, giving honour and reverence to the Blessed Sacrament, so that no-one may doubt the presence of the Lord and the adoration which is given to him in the reserved Sacrament. By its position and decoration it should be clear that this is a more important space than any others used for devotion (for example the shrine of a saint or a Lady chapel), and should demonstrate the close relationship between the eucharistic Liturgy and the reservation which derives from that action. A position adjacent to or close to the sanctuary will often meet the requirement for being 'truly pre-eminent' (HCWE, 9). Although closely linked, these two places, one for celebration of the Eucharist, the other for reservation, should be differentiated in such a way that the purpose of each is clear.

274. The *Order for the Blessing of a New Tabernacle* states that the tabernacle is, as well as a reminder of Christ's presence, 'also a reminder of the brothers and sisters we must cherish in charity, since it was in fulfilment of the sacramental ministry received from Christ that the Church first began to reserve the Eucharist for the sake of the sick and dying' (BB 1192). Themes and motifs used in the art and embellishment of a place of reservation should reflect these pastoral concerns as well as doctrinal ones.

If a Chapel formerly dedicated to a saint is to be used as the place of reservation it may be thought necessary to remove former fixed furnishings or stained glass, provide new furnishings on a eucharistic theme or make other alterations to the fabric. If such a chapel is of architectural or historic importance, the help of the Diocesan Art and Architecture Committee and Liturgy Committee should be sought, and, where listed, a faculty from the Historic Churches Committee will be necessary.

Provision for those praying

275. A principal advantage of a Blessed Sacrament Chapel is that it provides a quiet place in which the faithful may gather close to the reserved sacrament for times of private prayer and adoration. The design of the chapel should ensure that proper space is provided for the provision of chairs and kneelers for this prayer. (GIRM 315; RDC 79-82; HCWE 9; EM53; CB 910-913, RS 130) Especially if the chapel is relatively small, it is important that free space be provided for manoeuvring a wheelchair in and out of the chapel. It may be appropriate for this chapel to be carpeted. In some circumstances it may be possible to keep a separate chapel open for prayer during the day even if the main body of the church has to be kept locked.

10. Prayer and devotional space

276. *Around your throne*
the saints,
our brothers and sisters,
sing your praise for ever.
Their glory fills us with joy,
and their communion with us in your Church
gives us inspiration and strength,
as we hasten on our pilgrimage of faith,
eager to meet them.

Preface of All Saints, RM

277. As well as the place where the Christian community gathers to celebrate the sacraments, the church building is a place for the devotional and private prayer of her members, primarily through their prayer before the Blessed Sacrament (see section 9) but also through praying the Stations of the Cross, and veneration of saints, both local and universal.

Traditionally images of the Lord, the Virgin Mary and the Saints may be displayed in sacred buildings for the veneration of the faithful (GIRM 318). Images of the Saints remind the community that it is part of a greater body, the Church on earth and in heaven, made up of all those who have 'gone before us marked with the sign of faith' (RM, Eucharistic Prayer I). All are pilgrims as the Church journeys towards the heavenly city; by venerating the Saints the church in a particular place hopes for their prayers and companionship on the journey, and believes that we, too, may be transfigured as we celebrate the Liturgy of heaven united with all the Saints and angels.

Images may be in the form of statues, stained glass, paintings, textiles, ceramics or other good quality permanent representations. Since they are not simply representations or reminders, they should be of such a quality in design and manufacture as to convey something of the mystery towards which they lead the faithful. In general, mass-produced images are not suitable for this purpose.

278. Such images, which may be set in particular areas or shrines within the church, should not dominate or distract people during the Liturgy but instead lead the faithful towards a deeper participation in it. Consequently a side altar or shrine should never be more of a focus than the altar of celebration and the sanctuary area, nor should it intrude on that area in any way.

Images may be blessed according to the rite provided in the *Book of Blessings.*

Icons are not just holy images. A distinctive theology and spirituality of icons exists and should be considered and respected especially when icons are to be introduced into a church.

279. When considering the placing and decoration of images for veneration the following should guide the discussion:

- whether the proposed saint is a focus for the devotion of the whole local community;
- the beauty and dignity of the proposed image, including how it will complement the architecture and existing images in the building;
- how images which are no longer the focus of devotion may be disposed of reverently;
- what diocesan, statutory and other bodies will need to be consulted if the disposal of an image of historic or artistic value is contemplated;
- as a rule there should be only one image of any given saint in a church (GIRM 318).

280. *The Virgin Mary* Next to the place of the Blessed Sacrament, the Lady Chapel or image of the Blessed Virgin Mary is usually the most popular place in the church for personal devotion. Where possible, suitable seating and kneelers should be provided for the faithful to pray.

281. Among a parish's images, particular prominence should be give to the *patron of the church*. In considering what other images should be presented for devotion within the church it is necessary to maintain a proper balance between devotions common to the universal Church and those proper to the local church. Individual churches or families of religious should show a special honour to those saints who are properly their own (*General Norms for the Liturgical Year and the Calendar* (GNLY) 49).

A parish may also need to respect the popular devotion of groups within the parish being particularly sensitive to immigrant or ethnic groups. The shifting nature of both the community and popular devotions means that caution should be exercised before introducing permanent images particularly for the use of such groups.

282. *Stations of the Cross* Traditionally these are placed along a processional route around the walls of the church building; this allows the faithful to walk the 'way of the Cross' with Christ as they meditate and pray, and allows for a procession when the Stations are celebrated in a large group. The traditional form of the way of the cross is retained as the typical form of this devotional exercise; however alternative forms of the ways of the cross derived more directly from the Gospel accounts of the Passion have been approved by the Apostolic See and publicly used by the Roman Pontiff (*Directory on Popular Piety* (DPP) 134).

283. *Candles/devotional lights* Candles are used at every liturgical service as a sign of dignity and of the festiveness of the celebration. (CTM 114) They are also used outside of the Liturgy as a symbol of private prayer and devotion.

As far as possible, and in every case except where there is a serious danger of arson, wax candles or votive lights, which give a natural and living flame and can be seen to be consumed as they burn, should be used for devotional purposes. They should be placed where there is no danger of their setting fire to any nearby combustible material, and should be safely out of the reach of small children. It is a sensible precaution to make a fire blanket available nearby.

Careful use of lighting, including the natural flame of candles and votive lights can considerably enhance the prayerful atmosphere of a shrine or the setting of an image. The use of fake 'candles' with wax or oil inserts, or electric lights should be avoided, as should the use of electric 'haloes'. (CTM 114)

11. Outside the church

284. *For the celebration of the Eucharist, the People of God normally are gathered together in a church or, if there is no church or if it is too small, then in another respectable place that is nonetheless worthy of so great a mystery... Sacred buildings...should, moreover, be truly worthy and beautiful and be signs and symbols of heavenly realities.*

GIRM 288

285. *Lord,*
from the beginning of time
your voice has called to us,
inviting us to communion with you
teaching us the mysteries of your life,
guiding us on the way to salvation.

With silver trumpets Moses summoned Israel
to gather as your people.
Now you are pleased that in the Church
the sound of bells should summon your people to prayer.

...May their voice direct our hearts toward you
and prompt us to come gladly to this church,
there to experience the presence of Christ,
listen to your word,
offer you our prayers,
and both in joy and in sorrow
be friends to one another.

Blessing of Bells, BB, 1320

286. *Grant that this cemetery,*
placed under the sign of the cross,
may, by the power of your blessing,
be a place of rest and hope.
May the bodies buried here sleep in your peace,

to rise immortal at the coming of your Son.
May this place be a comfort to the living,
a sign of their hope for unending life.
May prayers be offered here continually
in supplication for those who sleep in Christ
and in constant praise of your mercy.

Blessing of a Cemetery, BB, 1432

287. The church building is a sign in its local community: it is the place where Christians gather. On the most holy night of the Easter Vigil, they gather not inside the building but outside, around a large fire, and enter only when the light of Christ, the paschal candle, is carried inside to dispel the darkness.

The earliest churches included a courtyard or gathering space, often with a well or fountain, where people congregated before entering the *aula* or hall where the Eucharist was celebrated. It may be difficult, particularly in urban areas to create such a space outside the doors of an existing church, but every effort should be made to ensure that there is an area somewhere outside the building where at least some of the community may gather, for example on Palm Sunday, when palms are distributed and blessed, and at the start of the Easter Vigil when the church meets around the New Fire. Plans for new church buildings should include such a space as a matter of course, making provision for power points and microphone sockets.

A gathering space outside the church is also an important place for people to socialise before and after the Liturgy and, if there is space and the area is safe and secure, consideration might also be given to providing the church with external decoration to mark the liturgical seasons, for example an Easter garden, Advent wreath, Christmas crib, banners or posters. Local planning regulations should be consulted. In some places it may be possible or desirable to provide an external power source for such 'external art'.

Thought should be given to processional routes both around and into the Church, for use during the celebrations of Holy Week and the Triduum, already mentioned, and also during the celebration of *Corpus Christi*.

In addition, the outside of the church should be welcoming both to members of the parish community and people who do not belong to the Church. In practical terms this includes:

- Good access for people who are disabled and for prams and pushchairs. There should be a ramp and handrails for people with disabilities and pushchair access to the main doors, and steps should be marked for those who are visually impaired.
- Safe access for large numbers of people, for example during the processions on Palm Sunday or at the Easter Vigil.
- Useful information (name or dedication of church, times of services, name and contact number of priest or parish office) on display.

- If there is space for parking by the church, spaces for disabled and parent/child parking should be allocated. At the main door of the church there should be adequate space for the arrival of wedding and funeral parties and for emergency access.
- If necessary, city-centre churches may need to negotiate reserved street parking with the local authority and request road markings to keep emergency accesses clear.

Cemeteries

288. The provision of cemeteries ensures a place for the reverent disposal of the mortal remains of the deceased. They also serve the important function of providing a focus for the community's remembering and praying for the dead, not only those of the immediate (blood) family, but of the wider family of the Church.

Those churches which have their own cemeteries adjacent to the church building must take responsibility for the proper maintenance of the grounds, and for ensuring the safety of any monuments and tombstones.

When building a new church, consideration might be given to the provision of a new cemetery, or at least to the need for proper facilities for the burial of the ashes of those cremated. Many churches have provided columbaria or burial grounds for this purpose. Prior permission should be sought from the appropriate Diocesan authorities. Guidance on this matter should be sought from the Liturgy Commission.

In more recent years there has been a growing trend to 'green' or 'woodland' burials. The provision of a burial site of this sort offers many advantages in terms of landscaping.

In England and Wales, since the 19th Century a system of perpetual lease has been instituted for many graves. This was not the previous custom of the Church, which has generally allowed the reuse of graves, with the removal to a charnel house of any remains uncovered when preparing the grave for reuse. At the present time the demand for 'new' graves, and the scarcity of available land, is such that consideration once more needs to be given, after an appropriate period of time, to the reuse of graves, with remains uncovered in the process of preparing a new burial either removed to another place, or buried at a deeper level.

When changes are contemplated to a cemetery, the archaeology of the site, and the possible artistic and historic value of monuments, should be considered. If human remains are to be moved, official permission is required. Moving gravestones will require that the views of those descendants who can be contacted must be sought. In all cases of work to cemeteries, a complete record of grave sites and inscriptions, etc., must be made and retained in the parish archive.

A Cemetery may be blessed according to the rite provided in the *Book of Blessings*.

Towers and Bells

289. Towers enhance the sign value of a building, and are a way of providing a visual reminder of Christ and the Church over an extended area. Towers need not be integrated into the church building, nor need they have internal rooms or spaces. However, they should clearly be part of the overall design.

Bells

290. The ringing of bells provides an aural reminder of Christ and his Church: calling people to the Liturgy, prompting people to pray at significant times of the day (Angelus), tolling as a sign of remembrance for the dead and ringing out in times of joy and celebration, of weddings and times of national and local celebration.

Bells may be blessed according to the rite provided in the *Book of Blessings*.

12. Works of art

291. *Consequently, the Church constantly seeks the noble assistance of the arts and admits the artistic expressions of all peoples and regions. In fact, just as she is intent on preserving the works of art and the artistic treasures handed down from past centuries and, insofar as necessary, on adapting them to new needs, so also she strives to promote new works of art that are in harmony with the character of each successive age.*

On account of this, in commissioning artists and choosing works of art to be admitted into a church, what should be required is that true excellence in art which nourishes faith and devotion and accords authentically with both the meaning and the purpose for which it is intended.

GIRM 289

292. *Church decor should contribute toward the church's noble simplicity rather than ostentation. In the choice of materials for church appointments there should be a concern for genuineness of materials and an intent to foster the instruction of the faithful and the dignity of the entire sacred place.*

GIRM 292

293. *In order to communicate the message entrusted to her by Christ, the Church needs art. Art must make perceptible, and as far as possible attractive, the world of the spirit, of the invisible, of God.*

Pope John Paul II, Letter to Artists, 12

294. In the Liturgy there are many places where works of art are used, worn, seen, touched or held. In addition to vestments, vessels, and books, there are items of furniture, fixtures and fittings, statues, mosaics and banners, shrines and reliquaries, and indeed the constituent parts of the building itself, in the materials and design of its windows, walls, ceilings, floors and doors. The design and fashioning of even the most functional item may provide an opportunity for a human being to co-operate with the Creator in a work of art. The expression of faith in such works of art has enriched Christian worship in England and Wales since the earliest days of the Church here.

295. Each community is called on to engage with and make its own the faith of the Church handed on to it. It will do this according to the genius of its members, and the genius of its time and place. It is appropriate therefore that the art works it commissions will express the experience in the modes of contemporary expression.

296. The process of commissioning a work of art can be exciting and fruitful both for the parish and for the chosen artist. A successful commission will add immeasurably to a church. Artists should be encouraged to spend time with the community as well as time in the church itself where the work will be placed. The artist should be carefully briefed before work begins. Assistance in this matter should be available from the Diocesan Art and Architecture Committee.

Beauty, goodness and truth are to be the primary aims in the creation of works of art for the church.

Accordingly, natural materials and specially commissioned works are to be preferred, wherever possible, to commercial or mass-produced items. Care in understanding a community's resources and needs will be required in making decisions as to how to proceed.

297. *The role of the artist* The artist's role is to use his or her gifts to lead the faithful into the liturgical celebration or into the mystery beyond the devotion it serves: 'The icon is venerated not for its own sake but points beyond to the subject which it represents' (John Paul II, *Letter to Artists*, 7). It is never a question merely of decoration; the artist's work expresses in a visual way aspects of spirituality and Church teaching in a way words cannot. The artist's responsibility is to consider how the work of art may contribute to the whole church building, and to the spirituality of the community with integrity; this does not necessarily mean working in a style which matches the building; churches in England and Wales are places where the artistic styles of one age sit alongside those of another, demonstrating the faith of generations.

298. *Where to find suitable artists* The Diocesan Art and Architecture Commission should make a list of artists. Although these are by no means the only people who may be approached, such a list can provide a useful starting point, and indicate places where the works of particular artists may be seen *in situ*. However, the long tradition of skilled artisans making items for their own parish church should not be ignored.

299. In many parishes, individuals and groups produce '*temporary artwork*' to celebrate a particular season or event, which is prepared, displayed and taken down over a relatively short period. Such items might include banners, posters or sculpture. While this type of artistic involvement is often based on good catechetical and liturgical practice there are a number of guidelines which might usefully be followed:

- all artwork, whether temporary or permanent, should be placed in an appropriate setting within the church, with due reverence to sacred objects and furnishings. Artworks should not be affixed to the altar, ambo, chair, tabernacle or font. It should not obscure the view of the assembly;
- the style, scale and materials used should be appropriate to the surroundings and the items themselves should be sufficiently well-crafted so that they do not fall apart while on display;
- from time to time there should be a regular review and 'weeding' of temporary artwork; in most situations the items have been prepared for a particular event or season and are not so relevant at other times. In addition, much temporary artwork does not store well, and does not add to the beauty of the church if it is taken out for second, third or subsequent years;
- caution is needed if temporary artwork puts vulnerable groups or individuals at risk – named photographs of the communion group, for example;
- in affixing temporary artworks to the fabric of a church, fixings should not irreversibly damage or mar wall surfaces. Advice should be sought from the Diocesan Art and Architecture Committee and, in the case of a listed church, a faculty for such fixings will be necessary from the Historic Churches Committee.

300. *Disposal of works of art*

A time of reordering or rebuilding is often a time for a parish community to examine the works of art which have been collected in the church since it was built, which may be of varying quality. The quality and condition of an item, however, does not necessarily have a bearing on the devotion inspired by it and a proposal to replace one image with another – even of the same saint – will often be fiercely opposed. This is a matter for the parish community, in consultation with the Bishop and his art and architecture commission, and with the Historic Churches Committee, in the case of a listed church building.

301. The Church is responsible for the safekeeping and maintenance of its patrimony (cf. 352–358). The removal, relocation or disposal of any historic or artistically important item is a matter both for the parish or community and the Diocese. The Diocesan Art and Architecture Committee should always be consulted on matters relating to relocation, removal or disposal, and also the conservation of objects in need. If an item of this kind has been given to the church, it would be courteous to seek the donor's view. In the case of fixed items within listed buildings, Historic Churches Committee involvement may also be necessary. Reference should be made to 'A Memorandum on the disposal of items from churches' (Appendix C).

302. *Inventory*

Parishes should keep an up to date inventory and photographic record of all their sacred vessels, vestments and other liturgical and devotional furnishings. If any item is loaned to another church, a record should be kept of this (cf. 104 above).

13. Vestments and linen

Vestments

303. All liturgical ministers have a responsibility to dress in a way which will add to the dignity of the celebration and which will not distract people from the celebration.

Vestments worn by deacons, priests and bishops should be made from good quality fabric in keeping with the dignity of the Liturgy. They should be of beautiful design and material, and do not require additional decoration; if there is to be decoration it should consist 'only of symbols, images or pictures representing the sacred' (GIRM 344).

At least some of the vestments worn in a particular church should be in keeping with the tenor of the building, and this should be considered when new vestments are being bought or commissioned.

Vestments should be worn with dignity; in particular, albs (or cassocks, if worn by servers) should be long enough for the minister concerned. All vestments should be carefully stored and cleaned when necessary.

For more details see GIRM 335-347.

304. Vestments of precious fabric or historic or artistic importance should be stored flat with a minimum of folding, cushioned appropriately to prevent cracking or bending of metallic threads. Such precious vestments should be used from time to time, according to the provisions of GIRM 346g.

Where precious or historic vestments need restoration or conservation, professional advice should always be sought. The Diocesan Art and Architecture Committee should be consulted.

If for some pressing reason, historic or precious vessels or vestments have to be disposed of, the advice of the Diocesan Art and Architecture Committee and Diocesan property service must be taken. See Appendix C below.

305. *Altar linen*

Altar linen should be white and spotlessly clean. (CTM 113) *Altar cloths* should be of a shape, size, and decoration in keeping with the design of the altar and its *mensa* (GIRM 304). Fussy lace or draperies should be avoided; 'noble simplicity' should be the aim.

14. SACRED VESSELS AND OTHER ITEMS

306. Materials and objects used in the celebration of the Liturgy are to be 'truly worthy and beautiful', authentic in their noble simplicity, and well adapted to sacred use (GIRM 288, 325, 326). The greatest care and sensitivity are necessary, even in minor matters, to achieve 'a noble simplicity and elegance' (GIRM 351, CTM 106).

Sacred vessels

307. Vessels for the eucharistic elements should be made of worthy and durable materials, their form should be in keeping with local culture and their function in the Liturgy (GIRM 329, CTM 108, RS 117).

308. The design of all such vessels should take into account:

- the liturgical setting in which they will be used. Whether the design is chosen to complement or contrast the setting, it should always be chosen with it in mind;
- their fitness for purpose. The fundamental eucharistic symbolism of the many sharing in the one bread and one cup is more clearly expressed when all the bread is contained in a single vessel and all the wine in one cup. Additional vessels may be necessary for the distribution of communion and may be brought to the altar at the breaking of the bread (CTM 109);
- vessels for the body of Christ preferably have the form of plates or shallow bowls rather than of cups or reliquaries;
- the chalice(s) should be of a capacity suitable for the congregation gathered. They should be easy for ministers to hand to communicants and vice versa, and be easy to drink from. Consideration should be given to sufficient chalices of a single design being provided for use on larger occasions – Easter liturgies, Midnight Mass.

The needs of the community are likely to be most appropriately met when its Eucharistic vessels are commissioned and designed for that specific community. Recourse to the catalogues of church suppliers should generally be taken as a last resort.

Sacred Vessels should be blessed according to the rite provided in the *Book of Blessings*.

Other items

309. Other liturgical vessels such as jugs or decanters, and lavabo bowls, should be suitable for their purpose, simple and pleasing in design, and should be kept spotlessly clean (CTM 110).

310. The Liturgy of the Easter Vigil brings its own special demands – the provision of a brazier to safely contain the large Easter Fire, a worthy stand for the Paschal Candle, a vessel for blessed water (when the font is not used). All these need to be worthy of their purpose.

The Paschal candle itself should be worthy of the great symbolism invested in it. It should not be small or mean. It should be appropriately decorated, but not so extensively that it ceases to resemble a candle. It needs to be lit and extinguished regularly through the Easter season and the year: safe means for this should be provided.

The Paschal candle is placed in different parts of the Church at different times of the year – on the sanctuary during Easter, in the Baptistery during the rest of the year, except during funeral liturgies when it is placed at the head of the coffin. It is not necessary that the same candle stand be used in all three locations. A smaller more easily portable stand will often be more serviceable for funerals, and a sconce may serve very well in the baptistery. However in all cases the candle stand must be worthy of this candle and the significance it bears (CTM 116).

15. Other spaces: sacristies, storage, toilets

311. Preparation is necessary for good liturgical celebration; in addition, the building requires a certain amount of cleaning and maintenance in order to provide a welcoming place of prayer and celebration for the Church. The reordering of a church may provide the opportunity to re-examine the provision of sacristies, working areas and storage.

312. *The sacristy* is where liturgical books, sacred vessels and vestments are made ready for use in celebrations. It should be large enough for the priest and ministers to vest in comfortably and prepare for the Liturgy, as well as allowing for any necessary briefing of the various ministers of the Liturgy.

Wherever the sacristy is situated in the building there should be a clear processional route from it to the main door of the church and to the sanctuary. A sacristy directly adjacent to the sanctuary rarely offers such a good processional route.

In the design of a sacristy careful consideration should be given to child protection issues.

313. *A sacrarium* should be provided for the reverent disposal of holy water (GIRM 334). This is a small sink which drains directly into the earth. For convenience, it is generally located in the sacristy. It should be appropriately labelled.

314. *A 'working sacristy'*, flower room or utility room where items may be cleaned, flowers arranged, and cleaning and other materials stored, is essential; it should have a sink with hot and cold running water and adequate working surfaces, cupboards and shelves for storage.

315. *Storage* There should be secure and accessible storage for vestments, sacred vessels, bread and wine, books, candles, and all the things needed to celebrate the seasons:

- for some items, for example vessels, monstrances, pyxes, microphones, a safe is necessary, fixed securely to the floor and/or wall;
- for other precious items, such as the Missal, Gospel book and Lectionaries, a locked cupboard may be advisable;
- Altar wine and bread should be kept in a cool, dry place; bread should be stored in a sealed container out of the reach of rodents or insects;
- vestments should be hung on hangers of appropriate size and shape; vestments and linen should be stored away from damp, dust and sunlight (See 304 above for guidance on the storage of precious and historic vestments);
- liturgical items not in daily use should be kept in a cupboard or storeroom;
- lockable storage for music, stands, choir robes (if worn) and amplification equipment should also be considered.

316. *Boiler/utility rooms, controls for sound, heating, lighting, etc* – If access to these is in or near the sacristy for convenience, care should be taken to prevent unauthorised access or tampering. Fire regulations forbid the use of boiler rooms for storage. Emergency routes/exits should not be obstructed.

317. *Washrooms* So far as is possible, lavatory and washing facilities should be provided for all who use the building, including infants and disabled people.

Adding such provision to existing churches usually poses a challenge. The advice of the Diocesan Art and Architecture Committee should always be sought, together with the involvement of the Historic Churches Committee in the case of listed buildings.

16. LIGHTING

318. Skilled arrangement of lighting can enhance the environment for worship by helping people focus on the liturgical action and reflecting the liturgical season and mood. This may be achieved by the use of different types of lighting for different parts of the church - spotlights, uplighters, and 'task' lighting. For example, it may be better that the lighting of the tabernacle is of a different type from that lighting the pages of the Lectionary on the ambo. The requirements of liturgical seasons should also be taken into account when designing a lighting system. For example, at the beginning of Easter Vigil, when the church is required to be in darkness, it should be possible to switch off all the lights of the church, and later turn on as many as are required from central controls. Other occasions require the lighting of just a particular part of the church, and perhaps in subdued rather than in full light.

Church lighting should be on the basis of a single scheme capable of variation to accommodate the various uses of the church building. Where historic or artistically important lighting fixtures exist, these should be retained as part of such a scheme. Diocesan Art and Architecture Committee and (where necessary) Historic Churches Committee involvement should be sought.

319. There should be suitable lighting for all the main places of liturgical activity: sanctuary, chair, ambo, altar, font, place of musicians and so on, which should be designed to illuminate the ministers and their actions without casting distracting shadows.

320. The lighting should enable the members of the assembly to recite and sing those parts of the Liturgy which belong to them and to move about in safety.

321. Consideration should also be given to the external lighting of the church grounds and access points to provide both safe access (for example, security lights in car parks) and security (for example, movement sensitive lights over the entrance doors). Floodlighting of the church, or of particular features of it, can assist in making the existence of the church better known, a reminder of the community of faith that it houses.

322. Light fittings should not be obtrusive and should be sympathetic to the style of the building. Thought should be given to maintenance programmes for the replacement of light bulbs.

323. A lighting engineer will be able to give advice on the characteristics of various systems. Some lamps, for example, take time to reach full brightness and should not be switched on and off repeatedly.

324. If a building is listed, plans for new lighting must be submitted to Historic Churches Committees, in the same way as other changes to the building.

325. In all cases, professional guidance should be obtained from the diocesan Property Services agency.

17. Sound Amplification

326. In all but the very smallest churches it will be necessary to provide some amplification for at least the presider and the readers, and perhaps also for the cantor and other musicians.

327. A loop system will enable those with hearing aids to take a fuller part in the celebration. A notice at the entrance should advise that there is a loop system and how to access it.

328. Microphones should be unobtrusive and their use should be flexible; there should be points provided at appropriate places within the church (for example, in the baptistery, in the sanctuary, close to the musicians, and by the main door). Provision should also be made for supplying amplification facilities outside of the church, (for example, at the place of assembly for the Procession of Palms and for the Easter Fire). They should be adjustable for all users, including children. The microphone at the ambo should be suitable for use by more than one reader at once, for example during the reading of the Passion narratives in Holy Week. The use of radio-microphones can lessen the need for many microphone points, and the use of voice-activated microphones can reduce the danger of a minister going unheard.

329. Training should be provided for all who will use microphones, for example priests, deacons, readers, musicians, pastoral assistants. Such training should normally form part of readers' training courses. Even when a person is invited to read without having completed such a course they should have practised at the ambo with the microphone before exercising their ministry in the Liturgy.

330. Where musical instruments are to be amplified, a system specifically for them should be considered, as the sound frequencies involved are at a different level from those used by speakers and singers. The services of the Diocesan Music Commission or other experts should be sought. (See also paragraphs 141–154)

331. Whenever an amplification system is being installed or modified, professional guidance should be obtained. Sensitivity both in design and fixing of such a system should be shown. The Diocesan Art and Architecture Committee and, where necessary, the Historic Churches Committee should be consulted. Guidance should also be obtained from the Diocesan Property Services agency.

18. Heating

332. The church should be efficiently heated to a comfortable but not excessive degree. How this is achieved will depend on local factors; however, in general efforts should be made to conserve heat when possible and to use energy wisely. The opportunity to use ecologically sensitive forms of power and heating should be explored.

333. It is worth considering providing an independent means of heating sacristies and working areas, so that people preparing for Liturgy, for example flower arrangers, musicians or sacristans are not required to work or rehearse in a cold, empty church or that there is need to provide full heating for the whole building at such times.

334. Adequate natural ventilation should also be provided.

335. Particularly where a church is on a busy road, or under a flight path and it is too noisy to leave doors and windows open, it may be necessary to install an air cooling system for use during the summer months.

336. Any proposed changes to the heating and ventilation of a church of architectural or historic interest should be explored in the first instance with the diocesan art and architecture or Liturgy commission who may need to seek further advice. Permission for any changes to a listed building will need approval by the Historic Churches Committee.

19. SECURITY

337. It is unfortunately very difficult for every church to be kept open for prayer all the time. However an open church is a sign of welcome by the Christian community. That sign of welcome can be enhanced when the parish can maintain a rota of people present in the church when it is open, offering a ministry of hospitality to visitors as appropriate. In the absence of any such arrangement the placing of security sensors in relevant places might permit the church safely to be left open. Where the whole church cannot be kept open a parish might be able to offer limited access for people's private prayer and for access to parish notices and times of services, for example to an open porch or side chapel. Each community has the responsibility of making its own assessment of what level of access to its church it can safely provide, and how to go about doing that, showing care for its mission, its people and its buildings.

338. Where there are people working alone in the church, sensible safety measures should be provided. In some situations it may be appropriate to install a 'panic button' in a sacristy or reconciliation room so that it is possible to summon help if necessary.

339. People working alone in the church should have clear instructions on which door to leave by, so that they do not leave the building vulnerable. Self-closing doors should be properly maintained.

20. Safety and Fire Regulations

340. In addition to legal requirements, the Church has a duty of care to all who use the church building. This includes keeping the building clean and in good repair, clearly marking hazards such as changes of level or protrusions, and not blocking access routes. Children should be adequately supervised. A First Aid box should be available for minor injuries.

341. Although when they are used for worship churches are exempt from the fire regulations governing public places, when they are used for other events regulations, covering fire exits, signs, seating and other areas may come into force.

Even if the church is only ever used for worship it is good pastoral practice for standard fire regulations to be taken note of and used for guidance, where appropriate. Care should be taken that the fire exit signs are not sited too obtrusively, or in places detrimental to historic fabric, although it should be realised that they will not fulfil their function if they are not sufficiently obvious to those using the church.

Suitable fire extinguishers and blankets should be sited at known points in the church building.

Part Four

Continuing care of Churches and their contents

Building Maintenance

342. The care and conservation of churches is an important matter, and requires careful and skilled management.

343. Church maintenance is very often delegated to those who have little experience of the maintenance of large public buildings. Yet the scale of necessary works in a church is very different to what is normal in the domestic setting. For example, changing light bulbs at home might simply require getting step ladders out, but in many churches it can require the erecting of scaffolding or the hiring of an elevated platform or 'cherry-picker'. Not recognising the difference can lead to infringement of best health and safety practice, as well as, often, the incurring of considerable additional expense. Early consultation with Diocesan Property Services on any matters to do with maintenance should ensure that the parish has easy access to those with professional experience in the proper maintenance of a large public building.

344. It is important that those entrusted with duty of care for a building consider the long term life of the building. What today can seem like short cuts and economies concerning maintenance frequently turn out to have substantial cost penalties further down the line. Care should be taken to ascertain, for example, from Diocesan Property Services departments, where it will be helpful to seek additional expert advice. In the case of historic or listed buildings, the Diocesan Art and Architecture Committee and Historic Churches Committee should also be consulted. Conservation is an essential element in maintenance and *vice versa*.

345. It is advantageous to ensure that there is a regular review of what works need attending to, and for a coordination of necessary works in order to minimise costs. Once the priorities for the repair, maintenance and conservation of a building's fabric have been decided on, a programme for the work can be established. With the aid of such a plan each element of the work can be costed, and the budget for this work coordinated with any other costs being incurred to meet other needs associated with the liturgical and pastoral life of the parish community.

346. Diocesan guidelines should be carefully observed with regard to the regularity and nature of building inspections. In general it is advised that a building receives a rigorous inspection, the Quinquennial inspection, every five years. This inspection should cover the roof and building fabric, glazing, electrical installation, heating, lighting, fire precautions and security issues. The subsequent report will identify the needs of the building fabric, and prioritise recommendations for repair and conservation works over the following five years. The regularity of such inspections is intended to ensure that any deterioration is identified in good time before significant damage has taken place. The pattern of inspection, and the programming of necessary works is also of assistance in the organising of fund-raising and in budgeting any necessary expenditure.

The Quinquennial Survey

347. The purpose of the survey is to assist those with responsibility of care for the building.

348. A few simple steps can ensure that the inspection is as thorough as it needs to be. A proper survey may take as long as a day to complete.

There should be clear records available of any recent previous inspections. Note should be kept of any ladders or specialist equipment needed to facilitate inspection of walls, windows, roofs and eaves. Full sets of keys should be available to provide access to all lofts, galleries, rooms and cupboards. The greater problems are often found in the more inaccessible places. It is therefore all the more important to ensure that these places are carefully inspected. It should be agreed before hand whether any equipment necessary to enable such inspection is to be provided by the parish or by the inspector.

349. The survey report is intended to accurately identify and describe matters that need addressing. It should make practical recommendations as to how problems might be overcome. The report should normally prioritise the works recognised as necessary. For example in the following manner:

- *Urgent work* – addressing matters which incur safety risk, fire risk, or structural risk;
- *Work required within two years* – addressing matters such as water ingress, dry rot, interior damage, security;
- *Work required within five years* – addressing matters such as structural movement, accelerating decay;
- *Desirable work* – decoration, improvements to fittings etc.

It is especially important that any recommendations concerning defects which constitute a safety hazard, or significant risk to the building fabric or its contents are clearly identified and promptly acted upon.

350. *The Annual Inspection*
It is only when faults have been identified that proper judgement can be exercised as to when and how they should be addressed.

351. Those with responsibility for care of the Church's buildings leave themselves hostage to fortune if they rely entirely on the Quinquennial inspection to identify defects and matters that need dealing with. A programme of monthly visual inspections of the building, and an annual programme for maintenance of building services both greatly help ensure that proper care is taken of the building and its contents. Guidance in developing such a programme can be obtained from the Diocesan Property Services department.

Care of our Cultural Heritage

352. The artistic patrimony of the Church is important. These works of architecture, painting, sculpture, together with the fittings and liturgical furnishings of churches, vestments and musical instruments, etc. are often an eloquent witness to the history and creativity of the Christian community (*c.f. The Inventory and Catalogue of the Cultural Heritage of the Church: A necessary and urgent task.* Pontifical Commission for the Cultural Heritage of the Church. Vatican City 1999, Introduction).

353. These cultural assets of the Church allow one to trace something of the way faith has come to different expression in the varied works of past generations. They reveal the creative capacity of artists, craftsmen and local guild traditions that has been able to give shape, colour and texture to the religious experience and devotion of the Christian community. They serve as witnesses to those individuals and communities who have gone before us - even artefacts of minor artistic merit witness in time to the effort of the community that has produced them and give a sense of the identity and 'reality' of such communities. Proper care must be taken to preserve, restore and protect this inheritance. The presence of such things in our churches remind us that we are part of a historical tradition – owing much to those who have gone before us, and with a responsibility for passing on the faith, and the things of faith, to those who will come after us.

354. The cultural assets of the Church belong to the Church, not just to a particular local congregation. Those who presently have direct and principal responsibility for their care cannot be considered in any sense their exclusive owner.

355. Those with present responsibility for these assets, also have a responsibility of making sure that they will be handed on to future generations. This patrimony is the tangible memory of evangelisation and inculturation, a valuable resource for catechesis and for the cultural life of the Church. The handing on of the patrimony of the Church is something important. Indeed it can be considered an essential link in the chain of tradition (*The Pastoral Function of Ecclesiastical Museums*, Pontifical Commission for the Cultural Heritage of the Church. Vatican City, 2001, 1.1).

356. In the particular case of church buildings and the environment for worship, the following items are of particular note:

- the building itself;
- liturgical fixtures – e.g. altar, ambo, chair, font, tabernacle, places for reconciliation;
- other fittings – e.g. altar rails, reredos;
- the organ and other 'fixed' musical instruments;
- vestments and sacred vessels, especially those of historic or artistic importance;
- statues and paintings;
- stained glass windows;
- pews;
- liturgical books;
- music books and sheets;
- church records, including photographs of church interiors, celebrations, ministers etc.

357. Particularly when there are plans to reorder a church, care should be taken to keep accurate photographic records of the previous arrangement.

358. Inevitably from time to time a tension will arise between the duty of care for an historic church and/or contents and the broader needs of the contemporary Church.

Whenever it is possible, and is compatible with the nature of present demands on a local Church community, the local community should exercise care for the patrimony entrusted to it. However when a local community is no longer able to exercise such care, it needs to consider how that responsibility might be exercised together with others, or even sometimes passed on to others. The local parish may find support from the Diocese of which it is part, or from other authorities in the local area. Sometimes funding may be available from national bodies. These avenues should be exhaustively explored before a parish considers asking the Diocese to recognise that any particular item is 'redundant' to its needs and seeking to transfer ownership elsewhere.

Guidance on applying for grants for the proper care and maintenance of buildings and contents is available from the Patrimony Subcommittee of the Bishops' Conference.

Appendix A

Liturgies and Space

The section includes a compilation of introductory and rubrical texts from the rites together with a brief commentary drawing out the spatial and kinetic dimensions of the celebration of these rites.

It provides an aide-memoire *for considering the demands of particular rites of the Church concerning the creation and use of various liturgical spaces. Still further guidance is available from the ritual book, especially from their General Introductions and rubrics, but also from the very language of the rites themselves.*

I Sacraments and other Rites

Rite of Christian Initiation of Adults

1. Rite of Acceptance Like a number of liturgical rites this begins at the entrance to the church in a place where people can gather.

> *The candidates, their sponsors, and a group of the faithful gather outside the church (or inside at the entrance or elsewhere) or at some other site suitable for this rite.*
>
> RCIA 48

All remain in place for the *Receiving the Candidates* until invited to 'come into the church, to share with us at the table of God's word.' (RCIA 60)

2. Dismissal of Catechumens Following the Rite of Acceptance, when the candidates are accepted into the Order of Catechumens, the candidiates are dismissed at the end of the Liturgy of the Word to reflect further on the Word until they are able to take part fully in the Eucharist at the Easter Vigil.

> *After the dismissal formulary, the group of catechumens goes out but does not disperse. With the help of some of the faithful, the catechumens remain together to share their joy and spiritual experiences.*
>
> RCIA 67A

In some parishes a room is set aside for this purpose and is sometimes referred to as a *Catechumeneon*. (See 158)

3. Scrutinies The three Scrutinies are celebrated on the Sundays of Lent. They 'are meant to uncover, then heal all that is weak, defective, or sinful in the hearts of the elect; to bring out, then strengthen all that is upright, strong, and good.' (RCIA 128)

> *After the homily, the elect with their godparents come forward and stand before the celebrant. ...The elect bow their heads or kneel.*
>
> RCIA 139

Space is required in front of the sanctuary and/or in the aisles for the Elect and their Godparents to stand and for the Elect to kneel, as required.

Easter Vigil see below.

Rite of Infant Baptism

4. There are four focuses of space with the Baptism Rite: *Entrance, Word, Font, Altar* and the rite envisages that the assembly will be able to process from one part of the building to another.

5. Reception of the Children The celebrating priest or deacon... goes to the entrance of the church or to that part of the church where the parents and godparents are waiting with those who are to be baptised (*Rite of Baptism for Children* (RBC) 35).

6. Liturgy of the Word The celebrant invites the parents, godparents and the others to take part in the Liturgy of the Word. If circumstances permit, there is a procession to the place where this will be celebrated, during which a song is sung (RBC 42).

7. Celebration of Baptism If the baptistery is located outside the church or is not within the view of the congregation, all go there in procession.

If the baptistery is located within view of the congregation, the celebrant, parents, and godparents go there with the children, while the others remain in their places.

If, however, the baptistery cannot accommodate the congregation, the baptism may be celebrated in a suitable place within the church, and the parents and godparents bring the child forward at the proper moment (RBC 51).

8. Concluding Rite Next there is a procession to the altar, unless the baptism was performed in the sanctuary (RBC 67).

Confirmation

9. The celebration normally takes place at the bishop's chair (cathedra). But when necessary for the participation of the faithful, a chair for the bishop should be placed in front of the altar or in some convenient place (CB 457).

After the Gospel the bishop and the priests who will be ministers of the Sacrament with him take their seats. The pastor or another priest, deacon, or catechist presents the candidates for confirmation, according to the custom of the region. If possible, each candidate is called by name and comes individually to the sanctuary. If the candidates are children, they are accompanied by one of their sponsors or parents and stand before the celebrant.

If there are very many candidates they are not called by name, but simply take a suitable place before the bishop (Rite of Confirmation 21).

Eucharist

There are no particular needs for a celebration of First Holy Communion. The needs for the celebration of Eucharist are covered in Sections 1–6. Particular issues relating to the ministering of Holy Communion are covered in paragraphs 216–217.

Reconciliation

See Section 8

Pastoral Care of the Sick

10. Anointing within Mass Although *Pastoral Care of the Sick* does not make any specific reference to liturgical space, it is important to be able to arrange the worship space so that where a number of people are to be anointed they are able to participate fully in the whole Liturgy from within the assembly. Sufficient space also needs to be provided for the priest to have easy access to those who are to be anointed.

Holy Orders

11. The celebration is to take place in the cathedral church, in a church of the home community of one or more of the candidates, or in some other important church. (Rites of Ordination *(*RO*) 108)*

The Ordination of one of its members is an important event in the life of any community but in the preparation consideration should be given to the question of whether the church is large enough for all, including concelebrating priests, to participate easily and fully.

The ordination should usually take place at the cathedra; but if necessary for the participation of the faithful, a seat for the Bishop may be placed before the altar or another, more suitable place.

*Seats for those to be ordained should be so placed that the faithful have a clear view of the liturgical rites. (*RO *116)*

Marriage

12. The rubrics to the rite anticipate that the Marriage Liturgy begins in a similar way to Baptisms and Funerals with the assembly, couple and guests being met at the door by the minister and all processing to the altar. A more common experience, suggesting a different meaning for this part of the Rite, is for the bride to enter on her father's arm and process to the altar, where the groom is already standing, to be greeted there by the celebrant. Both forms of entrance require an open processional route from door to altar and the former requires a gathering space at the entrance to the Church.

Like all participants the bride and groom are members of the assembly and where they sit should reflect this. Though they should be both visible and audible to the assembly during the Rite of Marriage at other times they should be able to listen to the readings and the homily, sing the acclamations and pray the Eucharistic prayer with the assembly.

Though the desire that all present should see the signing of the registers is appropriate this should not happen at the altar but at a suitably arranged table.

Funerals

13. The Funeral rites have three distinct stages: vigil, funeral and committal. In the various liturgies found in the *Order of Christian Funerals* (OCF) elements from the different stages are combined. In relation to the provision of spaces necessary to celebrate the Liturgy the most significant part is the reception which takes place at the Entrance of the church.

The Rite of Reception of the body is the first part of the funeral Liturgy at the church. Sometimes it is part of the principal funeral Liturgy; sometimes it is a separate rite. It begins, usually at the entrance of the church, with a greeting of the family and others who have accompanied the coffin. The minister sprinkles the coffin with holy water, taken from the font, in remembrance of the dead person's initiation and first acceptance into the community of faith. The entrance procession follows. The minister precedes the coffin and the mourners into church. The Easter candle will have been placed beforehand near the position to be occupied by the coffin. A white funeral pall, a reminder of the garment given at baptism, and therefore signifying life in Christ, may then be placed on the coffin by family members, friends, or the minister.

> *The Coffin should be placed before the altar, or in some other suitable place near it and in view of the congregation. If a catafalque is used, it should be of worthy design and harmonise with the sanctuary furnishings. Care should be taken that the placing of the catafalque and coffin does not impede either the view of the congregation or the movement of the people.* (OCF *142)*

In the Final Commendation at the end of the Funeral the coffin is sprinkled with holy water and incensed. The position of the coffin should allow for it to be easily walked around with a thurible.

Liturgy of the Hours

14. Parishes where Morning and Evening Prayer is regularly celebrated may wish to consider a separate space for celebration. For the Prayer of the Church a choral arrangement of seating (chairs facing each other) would be suitable in order to facilitate antiphonal recitation.

Liturgy of the Word with Children

15. Where this is part of a community's Sunday worship consideration could be given to its being afforded its proper space. The space should be safe and suitable for worship, accessible from the Church and with easy processional ways and ease of communication between the two worship spaces.

If no dedicated space is available, particular effort will have to be made to prepare such places as social clubs or parish hall for this worship. It would be unfortunate not to take the same care for the worship space provided for children as for adults.

II The Liturgical Year

Advent

16. Advent has a twofold character: as a time to prepare for the solemnity of Christmas when the Son of God's first coming to us is remembered; as a season when that remembrance directs the mind and heart to await Christ's Second Coming at the end of time. For these two reasons, the season of Advent is thus a period for devout and joyful expectation.

GNLY 39

17. Decoration The use of violet in Advent suggests a state of unfulfilled readiness and should no longer be regarded as an expression of penitence. It serves to set off the joyful white of Christmas with greater dramatic effect.

During Advent the playing of the organ and other musical instruments as well as the floral decoration of the altar should be marked by a moderation that reflects the character of this season, but does not anticipate the full joy of Christmas itself (CB 236, GIRM 305, 313).

18. Advent Wreath Where they are the custom, the Advent wreath and the Jesse tree, which help to sustain an expectant orientation toward Christmas, can assist the liturgical celebration and may be associated with the celebration of Mass.

The Advent Wreath is, however, primarily a domestic symbol. Where it is used in churches it should be of sufficient size to be visible but it should not obscure any of the primary places of liturgical action. Consideration may be given to hanging the wreath.

An Advent wreath should be safe and secure – candles should not be a fire hazard (particularly near resinous evergreens) or drip wax on floors. Stands should not be easily knocked over. Suspension points must be capable of bearing the (often considerable) weight and allow the candles to be lit and extinguished safely.

Customarily the Advent Wreath is constructed of a circle of evergreen branches into which are inserted four candles. According to tradition, three of the candles are violet and the fourth is rose. However, four violet or white candles may also be used.

The candles represent the four weeks of Advent and the number of candles lighted each week corresponds to the number of the current week of Advent. The rose candle is lighted on the Third Sunday of Advent, also known as Gaudete Sunday.

If the Advent wreath is used in church, it should be of sufficient size to be visible to the congregation. It may be suspended from the ceiling or placed on a stand. If it is placed in the presbyterium (Sanctuary), it should not interfere with the celebration of the Liturgy, nor should it obscure the altar, lectern, or chair.

BB, 1510-1512

Christmas

19. *Next to the yearly celebrations of the paschal mystery, the Church considers nothing more important than the memorial of Christ's birth and early manifestations. This is the purpose of the season of Christmas.*

GNLY 32

20. The Church celebrates the one true light, the light that banishes darkness.

- The Christmas image of light, of night giving way to day, is reinforced by the sequence of the Mass texts. Texts are provided for Christmas Masses in the evening (vigil), at midnight, at dawn, and during the day. The texts of these several celebrations are meant to be used at the actual time of day indicated by the titles of the celebrations.
- Symbols of the triumph of light over darkness and of life over death, for example, candlelight and evergreens, are traditionally used to decorate the church and assist devotion.
- The rich images of new light and new life provide many creative possibilities for decorating the church. The symbol of light recalls the Christian celebration of Easter and helps to link the incarnation with the paschal mystery of salvation.

Care should be taken when decorating the tree that such decoration is not unduly distracting from the main liturgical focuses. What may be quite acceptable in a domestic setting may well not be suitable for a place of worship.

21. Crib

In its present form the custom of displaying figures depicting the birth of Jesus Christ owes its origin to Saint Francis of Assisi who made the Christmas crèche or manger for Christmas Eve of 1223. However, as early as the fourth century representations of the nativity of the Lord were painted as wall decorations depicting not only the infancy narrative accounts of Christ's birth, but also the words of the prophets Isaiah and Habakkuk taken to mean that the Messiah would be born in the midst of animals in a manger.
If the manger is set up in the church, it must not be placed in the Sanctuary. A place should be chosen that is suitable for prayer and devotion and is easily accessible by the faithful.

BB, 1541, 1544

Epiphany

22. *The ancient solemnity of the Epiphany of the Lord ranks among the principal festivals of the whole liturgical year, since it celebrates in the child born of Mary the manifestation of the one who is the Son of God, the Messiah of the Jewish people, and a light to the nations... Hence: there will be a suitable and increased display of lights.*

CB 240

The custom of keeping Christmas decorations until Epiphany has been celebrated helps to show that Christmas and Epiphany are but two aspects of the same feast. It would be even more appropriate to extend this custom through to the celebration of the Baptism of the Lord, the close of the season of Christmas.

Lent

23. *Lent is a preparation for the celebration of Easter. For the Lenten Liturgy disposes both catechumens and the faithful to celebrate the paschal mystery: catechumens, through the several stages of Christian initiation; the faithful, through reminders of their own baptism and through penitential practices.*

GNLY 27

24. *Decoration* The use of violet vestments and the simplicity of decoration in the church reflect the penitential nature of this season.

25. *In Lent the altar should not be decorated with flowers, and musical instruments may be played only to give necessary support to the singing. This is in order that the penitential character of the season be preserved.*

On the fourth Sunday of Lent (Laetare Sunday), and on solemnities and feasts, musical instruments may be played and the altar decorated with flowers.

Paschale Solemnitatis (PS) 17, 25, (GIRM 305, 313)

Passion (Palm) Sunday 6th Sunday of Lent

26. *Commemoration of the Lord's Entrance into Jerusalem: The Procession* The Procession is the first option in the Roman Missal. The congregation assemble in a secondary church or chapel or in some other suitable place distinct from the church to which the procession will move.

To assist people to participate fully in this liturgical action consideration should be given to:

- audibility of presider and other ministers (it is likely that amplification will be necessary, especially if the place of assembly is out of doors and the number of people present is large)
- visibility of the presider and other ministers;
- the processional route; it should not necessarily be assumed that the shortest route is the best processional route. The meaning of procession includes the experience of shared journey.

The second option: The Solemn Entrance is held at the church door, inside the church or in another suitable place within the Church outside the Sanctuary. Again consideration should be given to:

- audibility;
- visibility.

27. Reading of the Passion Where the Passion is proclaimed by a number of voices consideration should be given to:

- where the individual readers will stand;
- the need for amplification and hence provision of microphone sockets or use of radio microphones.

Chrism Mass

28. Reception of Oils The oils blessed by the bishop can be formally received and welcomed by parish communities in the diocese. This may take place during an appropriate service at the end of Lent or as one of the preparation rites celebrated with the elect on Holy Saturday. Those who were present at the Chrism Mass may carry the oils in the entrance procession of the Evening Mass of the Lord's Supper, incense may be used, and a few words of reception spoken.

Easter Triduum

Holy Thursday

29. Washing of the Feet The rite of washing feet in memory of the action at the Last Supper takes place after the reading of the Gospel at the Evening Mass of the Lord's Supper. The rite calls for the placing in a suitable place of chairs for those whose feet are to be washed. There needs also to be room for the priest to kneel for the washing of the feet, and for the assistant ministers as they hold towels and jugs and bowls of water.

30. Altar of Repose The Mass of the Lord's Supper ends simply with the prayer after communion. The blessing and dismissal are omitted. The Mass is followed by the solemn transfer of the consecrated elements to the Blessed Sacrament chapel. The time for private adoration afterwards can help the faithful to experience the presence of the risen Lord in the three days of the paschal feast. The Triduum of waiting and praying has begun.

The rites presume that the Eucharist is normally reserved in churches in a separate Blessed Sacrament chapel. The procession with the Eucharist therefore leaves from the altar and goes to the reservation chapel, where the Liturgy ends. If a church does not have a Blessed Sacrament chapel, one should be set up for the occasion in the best way possible. Decorations are to be suitable and in due proportion.

Good Friday

31. Reading of the Passion

See 27.

32. Veneration of the Cross The veneration, which follows the Liturgy of the Word, focuses not so much on a figure of the crucified as on the cross itself; with lighted candles on each side, it is a symbol of victory and salvation. A large, well-crafted cross solemnly shown to the people provides a moving climax to the Liturgy of Good Friday. Each person comes forward after the showing to kiss or touch the cross in an individual gesture of veneration. Only one cross is used. If it is large enough and is set up in the midst of the assembly, processions of the faithful will be able to approach it from several directions at once. This personal act of participation is an important feature of the Liturgy. Simultaneous veneration by all should be used only when this individual gesture is impossible. The antiphons, Reproaches, or other songs that are sung during the veneration view the cross within the whole story of salvation and look to the light of the resurrection. They may be sung responsorially with the people.

Easter Vigil

33. Service of Light A large fire is prepared in a suitable place outside the church. As on Passion Sunday the following should be considered:

- a suitable place for gathering;
- audibility/amplification;
- clear processional route (cf. 26).

> *The Easter candle leads the procession and it is placed on a stand in the middle of the sanctuary or near the ambo.* RM, Easter Vigil 7

The Easter proclamation (*Exsultet*) is sung standing in the holy light of the Easter candle and the candles held by the people. For good effect, electric lighting may be left off until the service of light is finished. Then it could be used throughout the Easter Vigil, focusing first on the ambo, then on the font, and finally on the altar.

34. Liturgy of Baptism The first part of the Liturgy of Baptism takes place at the font, if it is visible. Otherwise a vessel of water is placed in the sanctuary. Consideration should therefore be given to:

- visibility of the font;
- adequate gathering space around the font for those to be baptised, and, where appropriate parents and godparents, candidates for confirmation;
- processional route to the font;
- audibility/amplification.

Confirmation is celebrated in the same place as baptism – that is, either in the baptistery or on the sanctuary.

If the blessing of the baptismal water does not take place at the baptistery, the vessel of water is reverently carried to the font after the renewal of baptismal promises. If the blessing of baptismal water does not take place, the water blessed for the renewal of baptismal promises is put in a suitable place after the renewal.

Easter

35. *The fifty days from Easter Sunday to Pentecost are celebrated in joyful exultation as one feast day, or better as one 'great Sunday.'*

These above all others are the days for the singing of the Alleluia.

GNLY 22

The paschal candle has its proper place either by the ambo or by the altar and should be lit at least in all the more solemn liturgical celebrations of the season until Pentecost Sunday, whether at Mass, or at Morning or Evening Prayer. After the Easter season the candle should be kept with honour in the baptistery, so that in the celebration of Baptism the candle of the baptised may be lit from it. In the celebration of Funerals the paschal candle should be placed near the coffin to indicate the death of a Christian is his own Passover. The paschal candle should not otherwise be lit nor placed in the sanctuary outside the Easter season.

PS 99

The tradition of celebrating baptismal vespers on Easter Sunday with the singing of psalms during the procession to the font should be maintained where it is still in force, and as appropriate restored.

PS 98

Ordinary Time

Presentation of the Lord (2nd Feb)

36. Encouragement is given on this day for the people to gather in a chapel or other suitable place outside the church where the Mass will be celebrated, and then with lighted candles enter the church (RM, 2nd February).

Corpus Christi

37. *Wherever it is possible in the judgement of the diocesan Bishop, a procession through the public streets should be held, especially on the Solemnity of the Body and Blood of Christ as a public witness of reverence for the Most Holy Sacrament, for the devout participation of the faithful in the eucharistic procession on the Solemnity of the Body and Blood of Christ is a grace from the Lord which yearly fills with joy those who take part in it'.*

RS 143

The Church's guidance for such processions is given in the ritual book *Holy Communion and Worship of the Eucharist outside Mass* (part of the *Roman Ritual*). It can be downloaded from www.liturgyoffice.org.uk

It will normally begin immediately after the celebration of a Mass. It should normally go from one church to another, but may return to the same church where it began.

When a public procession cannot be held, 'the tradition of holding eucharistic processions should not be allowed to be lost. Instead, new ways should be sought of holding them in today's conditions: for example, at shrines, or in public gardens if the civil authority agrees' (RS 144).

Well in advance of any planned procession, the appropriate permissions must also be obtained from any necessary civil authorities – for example the local council or police force for processions taking place on public roads. The civil authorities will indicate the necessary health and safety measures that should be observed for the well-being of worshippers and the general public.

Appendix B

General outline of steps and stages in a reordering or new-build project

NB Each diocese will have its own binding procedures that parishes are required to follow. However the outline below offers an indication of how those procedures will generally operate.

Sometimes the complexity of a particular project will mean that certain stages will need to be repeated a number of times before permission is granted to proceed to the next stage. Good consultation at the earliest stages will minimise the need for this.

A. Before obtaining plans or tendering for preparation of plans

- Preliminary consultation with diocesan bodies – e.g. Liturgy Commission, Art and Architecture Committee, Diocesan Property Services. The Historic Churches Committee should be consulted in all cases concerning listed churches and chapels.
- Consultation/Formation within parish.
- Identification of 'Stated Need'.
- Preparation of design brief against which architect/designer can prepare plans (it will generally be necessary to have this design brief reviewed and approved by the Liturgy Commission/Art and Architecture Committee).

B. Development and approval of plans

- Invitations to tender for work submitted to architect/designer approved by diocese.
- Plans obtained from architect/designer approved by diocese.
- Plans approved by parish.
- Plans submitted to Liturgy Commission/Art and Architecture Committee.
- Plans approved by Liturgy Commission/Art and Architecture Committee (in the case of listed buildings this will be subject to approval of Historic Churches Committee).
- [Plans submitted to Historic Churches Committee].
- [Plans approved by Historic Churches Committee].

C. Works planned and carried out

- Works schedule supervised by Diocesan Property Services.
- It is likely that the Liturgy Commission/Historic Churches Committee will wish to inspect work at different stages to ensure that it complies with the various requirements they will have specified.

Appendix C

A Memorandum on the Disposal of Objects from Churches

There may be various situations in which it is proposed to sell objects from churches:

- it may be seen as a way of raising funds for some project;
- it may be felt that unused objects are too expensive to store and insure, and are not 'earning their keep';
- if a church or religious institution is closed down or demolished it may be necessary to find new homes for objects.

These situations are obviously radically different. The purpose of this memorandum is to provide assistance for those who, as in the third case, are forced to dispose of objects; it is also hoped to dissuade those responsible from selling objects when this is not in fact inevitable.

Churches and their contents are an inheritance from the past of which we are merely the temporary custodians. We are indebted for them to past generations of the faithful who have dedicated them to God's service. We need to be very sure of our ground before we alienate them once and for all from that service. A less than responsible attitude towards our patrimony has within recent years become more widespread than ever, and the Church will be seen as behaving irresponsibly if it ignores it.

The sale of objects to raise funds may, in certain circumstances, be justifiable.

However, it has to be remembered that once the object is sold it is gone for good, and it will probably be impossible ever to recover it. There will probably be many other ways in which the money can be raised. Furthermore, feelings of guilt on the part of vendors too often cause them to sell objects in a manner which means that the best price will not be obtained.

Only too often parishioners are not consulted, or even informed; this leads to understandable resentment, especially when the donor or person commemorated is still remembered.

The problem of objects that are not used and are expensive to store and insure is often comparatively easy to solve. *The Circular Letter from the Sacred Congregation for the Clergy to the Presidents of the Episcopal Conferences, The Care of the Historical and Artistic Patrimony of the Church* (1971), stated:

> *"In the event that works of art and artistic treasures passed down to us from previous centuries are no longer considered in any way suitable for divine worship, they must never be relegated to profane use. They are to be kept in*

a fitting place, such as a diocesan or interdiocesan museum to which all who wish to view them can have access."

So far the only such museums in England and Wales are those at old-established institutions such as Saint Edmund's, Ware, Ushaw, Oscott and Stonyhurst. Some cathedrals, university chaplaincies etc. possess collections of miscellaneous items, despite the lack of facilities for their display. There is no reason why objects from Catholic churches should not be loaned to the treasuries which have been set up, with the aid of the Goldsmiths' Company, in several Anglican cathedrals. In fact the treasuries at Durham, York, Lincoln, Winchester, Gloucester and Canterbury are already showing Roman Catholic plate. Churches lending plate may borrow it back whenever they wish. It is equally possible for a wider range of objects to be loaned to local art galleries and museums: those already showing Roman Catholic objects include the Victoria and Albert Museum; the National Portrait Gallery; the Birmingham City Art Gallery; the Walker Gallery; the Ely Cathedral Stained Glass Museum; the Watford Museum; and the Bowes Museum.

Even objects of no intrinsic value, whether monetary or artistic, may have a strong claim to be retained, on the grounds of historical interest and educational value. The Challoner bicentenary exhibition at Westminster in 1981 demonstrated how effective even trivial objects can be in recreating the atmosphere of a past age of religion. A plaster Pietà with bleeding wounds can tell us more about a certain type of Catholic piety than any number of words.

It has been accepted that there will be cases in which objects from churches will have to be found new homes. In the first place, every effort should be made to relocate them in other churches or religious institutions, whether by gift, loan or sale. There is as yet no machinery within the Catholic Church in England and Wales for this; (for the Church of England scheme, see notes). However, notices can be inserted in the Catholic press, with encouragement from Diocesan Liturgy Commissions. Temporary storage, especially for larger objects, is a problem for which various solutions may be available (e.g. cathedral crypts).

Despite the foregoing, cases are bound to arise where it is decided that objects should be sold. The first question to be considered is that of ownership. It is widely held that the contents of parish churches and cathedrals are the property of the diocesan trustees, and that permission from the Vicar General is all that is needed for their sale. However, the 1983 Code of Canon Law states that 'under the supreme authority of the Roman Pontiff, ownership of goods belongs to that juridical person which has lawfully acquired them' (Canon 1256).

One of the consultors for the recent revision of Canon Law comments:

"Since the 'Catholic Church' has no legal existence under English Law as an owner of property, all our property has to be vested for legal purposes in some form of trust, and it is usual for all the property in a diocese, other than that of Religious, to be vested in a diocesan trust. The clergy get used to regarding the diocese as in some sense the owner or overlord, because all alienations of any substance have to be referred to the Bishop or Vicar General; but the real owner remains the canonical owner; and so, for example, the real owner of all the property of a parish is neither the parishioners nor the Parish Priest,

but the juridical person of the parish. Every diocese and every parish in it is a distinct juridical person with the capacity and right to acquire and possess property in its own name. A parish priest is simply the 'guardian' of the rights of his parish which he must safeguard in accordance with canon law."

Furthermore, Canon 1292 §2 states that:

"the permission of the Holy See also is required for the valid alienation of goods whose value exceeds the maximum sum, or if it is a question of the alienation of something given to the Church by reason of a vow, or of objects which are precious by reason of their artistic or historical significance".

Canon 1291, on the leave required for valid alienation, limits the requirements to:

"goods which, by lawful assignment constitute the stable patrimony of a public juridical person whenever their value exceeds the sum determined by law". (All parishes and dioceses are public juridical persons. Canon 515 §3 and Canon 372 §1 and Canon 373)

Canon 1293 §1 lays down the basic requirements for alienation, viz.

1. a just reason, such as urgent necessity, evident advantage, or a religious, charitable or other grave pastoral reason;
2. a written expert valuation of the goods to be alienated,

and §2 states that:

"to avoid harm to the Church, any other precautions drawn up by lawful authority are also to be followed".

It would appear, in view of the above, that, while in certain circumstances the permission of the Holy See is required for alienation, in all circumstances it is proper to obtain the agreement of the diocesan authorities, the Parish Priest, and the parishioners.

Once all the necessary permissions and agreements have been obtained, the question arises of how best to sell objects. One possibility is to make use of the system operated by the Church of England, which the Church Commissioners have generously agreed to make available (see the notes). It is recommended that in all circumstances those responsible should consult the Diocesan Liturgy Commission.

Expert opinion must be obtained (see above). If there are no suitable qualified experts known to members of the Diocesan Liturgy Commission, the Patrimony Committee of the Bishops' Conference could recommend names. These should be art historians or curators rather than dealers or auctioneers. In the case of objects of particular value, whether intrinsic (e.g. gold and silver plate) or artistic (e.g. objects designed by architects, original works of art), the opinion of experts should always be sought. They should be asked to give, first, their opinion on the provenance, history, and the artistic value of each object, and, second, their advice on how each object can be best disposed of.

The Code (Canon 1283) requires that every parish church should keep a proper inventory of its possessions. In practice, this rarely occurs. The National Association of Decorative and Fine Arts Societies has Church Recorders Groups throughout the country. They may be willing to make such inventories on a voluntary basis.

Notes

1. The Church Commissioners of the Church of England have established a system for disposing of the contents of redundant churches, or of superfluous contents from churches in use. They have generously agreed that it would be in the interests of all if the Church of England and the Roman Catholic Church could benefit from a common system.

2. In the Church of England the disposal of furnishings from redundant churches is in the first instance the responsibility of each diocese. Each Anglican diocese has appointed a Furnishings Officer to look after this work. Most officers are successful in disposing of contents without the assistance of the Commissioners. It is suggested that Roman Catholic dioceses might usefully establish contact with the officers of their Anglican counterparts.

3. The Church Commissioners circulate a 'Central Contents Register', listing items that cannot be disposed of locally. This is sent every two or three months to each diocese, as well as to certain individuals and organisations who have requested a copy. They also include requests received for particular items. Alongside each item is listed the name and address of the person with or requiring an article and it is asked that the person be contacted directly. The Commissioners do not themselves deal with the sale and purchase but leave it to the parties concerned. They do not repeat requests, unless specifically asked to do so, and they do not handle stained glass.

4. The Church Commissioners have kindly agreed that these lists should be circulated also to Roman Catholic dioceses, and they will include Roman Catholic items. Those wanting items included should contact the Church Commissioners Office (1 Millbank, London, SW1P 3JZ).

Adapted from *The Parish Church* (PC) – Bishops' Conference of England and Wales 1984 – Appendix B

ABBREVIATIONS

BB Roman Ritual, *Book of Blessings*, editio typica, 1984.

CB Congregation for Divine Worship, *Ceremonial of Bishops*, 14 September 1984.

CCC *Catechism of the Catholic Church*, 2nd edition, 2000.

CIGI Congregation for Divine Worship, *Christian Initiation*, General Introduction, 2nd edition typical, 1973.

CTM Catholic Bishops' Conference of England and Wales, *Celebrating the Mass*, 2005.

DPP Congregation for Divine Worship, *Directory on Popular Piety and the Liturgy: Principles and Guidelines*, 17 December 2001.

EM Congregation of Rites, Instruction *Eucharisticum mysterium*, on the worship of the Eucharist, 25 May 1967.

ES Congregation for Divine Worship, Decree. *Eucharisticae Sacramentum*, 21 June 1962: AAS 65 (1973).

GIRM Roman Missal, *General Instruction of the Roman Missal*, 20 April 2000.

GNLY Congregation of Rites, *General Norms for the Liturgical Year and the Calendar*, 21 March 1969.

HCWE Roman Ritual, *Holy Communion and Worship of the Eucharist outside Mass*, 21 June 1973.

ID Sacred Congregation for the Sacraments and Divine Worship, Instruction *Inaestimabile Donum* 3 April, 1980.

Letter Pope John Paul II, *Letter to Artists*, 4 April 1999.

LM Roman Missal, *Lectionary for Mass*, 2nd English edition, 1981, Introduction

MPM Catholic Bishops' Conference of England and Wales, *Music in the Parish Mass*, 1981.

MR Missale Romanum, *Missale Romanum*, editio tertia, 20 April 2000.

Nolan *The Nolan Report: A Programme for Action. Final Report of the Independent Review on Child Protection in the Catholic Church in England and Wales*, 2001.

OCF Roman Ritual, *Order of Christian Funerals*, Edition for England and Wales, 1990.

PC Catholic Bishops' Conference of England and Wales, *The Parish Church*, 1984.

PPG 15 Department of the Environment, *Planning Policy Guidance 15: Planning and the Historic Environment*, 1994.

PPG 16 Department of the Environment, *Planning Policy Guidance 16: Archaeology and Planning*, 1990.

PS Congregation for Divine Worship, Circular letter, *Paschale Solemnitatis*, 16 January 1988.

RBC Roman Ritual, *Rite of Baptism of Children*, 15 May 1969.

RCIA Roman Ritual, *Rite of Christian Initiation of Adults*, 2nd Edition for England and Wales, 1985.

RDA *Rite of Dedication of an Altar* in Roman Pontifical, *Rite of the Dedication of a Church and an Altar*, editio typica, 1984.

RDC Roman Pontifical, *Rite of the Dedication of a Church and an Altar*, editio typica, 1984.

RM Roman Missal, *Roman Missal*, England and Wales, 1974.

RO Roman Pontifical, *Rites of Ordination of Bishops, Presbyters, and Deacons*, second typical edition, 1993.

RP Roman Ritual, *Rite of Penance*, 2 December 1973.

RS Congregation for Divine Worship, Instruction *Redemptionis Sacramentum*, 25 March 2004.

SC Vatican Council II, Constitution on the Liturgy *Sacrosanctum Concilium*, 4 December 1963.

SS John Paul II, *Spiritus et Sponsa*, 22 November 2003.

VD Bishops' Conference of England and Wales, *Valuing Difference: People with disabilities in the life and the mission of the Church*, 1998.

For details of how to most easily access these various documents please visit www.liturgyoffice.org.uk/Resources/CFW

Acknowledgements

INDEX